THESE ARE OUR BODIES

FOR MIDDLE SCHOOL

Church Publishing
NEW YORK

LEADER GUIDE

Scripture taken from the Common English Bible®, CEB® Copyright © 2010, 2011 by Common English Bible.™ Used by permission. All rights reserved worldwide. The "CEB" and "Common English Bible" trademarks are registered in the United States Patent and Trademark Office by Common English Bible. Use of either trademark requires the permission of Common English Bible.

The scripture from the *New Revised Standard Version Bible (NRSV)* © 1989 by the Division of Christian Education of the National Council of Churches of Christ in the USA. Used by permission.

Scripture quotations marked *(NLT)* are taken from the Holy Bible, *New Living Translation*, copyright © 1996, 2004, 2007 by Tyndale House Foundation. Used by permission of Tyndale House Publishers, Inc., Carol Stream, Illinois 60188. All rights reserved.

Morehouse Education Resources,
a division of Church Publishing Incorporated
19 East 34th Street, New York, NY 10016
www.churchpublishing.org

Cover design by Jennifer Kopec, 2 Pug Design
Typeset by Progressive Publishing Services

ISBN-13: 978-1-60674-311-9 (pbk.)
ISBN-13: 978-1-60674-312-6 (ebook)

Printed in the United States of America

CONTENTS

PREFACE

The only way I know how to teach anyone
to love God, and how I myself can love
God, is to love what God loves, which is
everything and everyone, including you and
including me![1]

—Richard Rohr

We love because [God] first loved us.

—1 John 4:19, *NRSV*

If we love each other, God remains in us and
[God's] love is made perfect in us.

—1 John 4:12, *CEB*

....

1 Richard Rohr *Franciscan Mysticism: I AM That Which I Am Seeking* (Albuquerque, NM: Center for Action and Contemplation: 2012), disc 2; assessed https://cac. org/love-god-in-what-is-right-in-front-of-you-2016-01-17/, January 23, 2016.

Welcome to *These Are Our Bodies for Middle School Leader Guide.*

As parents, leaders, or clergy, you recognize the imperative to teach and lead young people in connecting their faith life and their sexuality. The church has something to say to our young people, with a message of empowerment and acceptance. The Church is called to assist people to grow in their faith and lead the life to which they are called. Considering anew what God is calling us toward, fostering respect, wholeness, and love will lift up the Body of Christ. Just as there are seasons to our faith (such as birth, baptism, and reaffirmation), there are seasons to our sexuality (birth, awareness, growth, change, and transformation). *Sexuality: A Divine Gift* explores the interplay of the physical experience, love, and gift:

> The Episcopal Church is a sacramental church. Anglicans claim a union of physical experience and inward grace both in the sacraments of the church and in our daily lives.
>
> The church increasingly understands that our sexuality is an important (though not the only) means by which we learn to be lovers. Our awareness of each other, our acceptance of our affection for each other as God's creations, and our delight in the special gifts that each of us brings to a relationship because of our sexuality—all these are evidence of the blessings that God intends for us in our dealings with each other.[2]

With all this in mind, *These Are Our Bodies* offers practical information, developmental material, and suggestions on how to ask and answer questions, all in the context of our faith as Christians, particularly as Episcopalians. *These Are our Bodies* was created in response to the need of The Episcopal Church for program resources to help young people explore sexuality in the context of a faith community. The program consists of a *Foundation Book* and a middle-school program that includes this *Leader Guide*, a *Participant Book,* and a *Parent Book*.

These Are Our Bodies: Sexuality & Faith at Church & Home, is the *Foundation Book* for the entire *These Are Our Bodies* program. Modules for a variety of age levels will be offered in subsequent years, with the first being this middle-school module published simultaneously with the *Foundation Book*. The *Foundation Book* is an integral part of the middle-school program. Facilitators, Small-Group Leaders, and parents are all encouraged to have a copy of the *Foundation Book*.

The *These Are Our Bodies Foundation Book* serves as a theological and practical guide to conversation about the complexities of sexuality in today's world, grounded in the Episcopal faith tradition. The book includes essays on the role of sexuality and practical guides to help inform church educators, clergy, parents, youth leaders, or anyone who seeks to broaden their knowledge on this subject. It is organized into four sections, The Theological, The Ethical, The Biological, and The Practical, each exploring the complexity of sexuality. The *Foundation Book* is written both to be read on its own and as part of the unified *These Are Our Bodies* program. The extensive annotated resource section and glossary round out the book to give readers the information they need for further exploration in areas around sexuality.

....

2 Education for Mission & Ministry Unit. *Sexuality: A Divine Gift* (New York: Domestic and Foreign Missionary Society, 1987), 4.

The theological chapters in Section I explore the dynamic of sexuality and its connection to our faith. This section concludes with a discussion of the role of the church in the area of sexuality and will be helpful to Facilitator and Small-Group Leaders of the middle-school program.

Section II, The Ethical, gives us a new language necessary to expand our view of sexuality. The binary concepts of sexuality as male or female, married or single, heterosexual or homosexual are expanding. Readers will receive a new way to understand sexuality, including new language that seeks to honor and respect the dignity of all people. An understanding of the Ethical chapters will inform Facilitators and Small-Group Leaders as they work with participants of the middle-school program.

In Section III, The Biological, we expand on the role of parenting in healthy development and provide a review of developmental theories, moral development psychology, and faith development across the lifespan. The research and theories of leading psychologists underpins our understanding of the needs of children, including the healthy growth of their bodies and their moral development. We conclude this section with a discussion of faith development and its implications in understanding the complexity of human sexuality, which is especially helpful to Facilitators and Small-Group Leaders in the middle-school program.

Section IV, The Practical, gives adults the tools needed to understand the stages of child development that inform our ministry with children and teens. The review of development (physical, emotional and social, spiritual, and moral) will benefit anyone working with or raising children and teens.

The annotated resource section and glossary are rich with valuable insights and materials. For Facilitators and Small-Group Leaders in the middle-school program the *Foundation Book* will be a resource linking faith and sexuality.

As a Church, we want to empower parents to be the primary sexuality educators of their children, walking with them on the journey and providing resources to assist them in having important and timely conversations. *These Are Our Bodies: Middle School Program* answers that request and this *Leader Guide* contains the background and sessions needed to plan and implement the program. The sessions in *These Are Our Bodies* program materials (age-based *Leader Guide, Parent Book,* and *Participant Book*) are each designed to teach concepts around our faith in ways that connect with young people and give them opportunities to strengthen their faith. The program includes content that makes a connection between our faith and sexuality, the modeling of Facilitator and Small-Group Leader interaction, how questions can be answered, and how to create a safe, educational atmosphere.

These Are Our Bodies for Middle School is a comprehensive faith and sexuality program that can be used in a array of settings and is adaptable to a meet the needs of a variety of groups. Based on the universal needs of young people and their parents, it honors and lifts up parents as the primary sexuality educators to their children by involving parents as an integral part of the experience. There is a parent-only session (Preview Session) and a parent and middle-schooler session (Session 8) to empower parents and children to have meaningful conversations around sexuality and faith.

This *Leader Guide* contains 10 sessions that are developmentally appropriate, creatively interactive, and faith-based. They place human sexuality in the context of faith. Direct and indirect teaching around concepts such as God's creation, scripture, and sexuality as gift from God are intertwined throughout the sessions. Conversations and teaching around the stewardship of gifts, responsible behavior, and God's grace and love are found throughout the sessions. Facilitators and Small-Group Leaders will find detailed planning information as well as the background and useful information to employ the program in your church or community.

Our hope is that this program will be a gift to you and the young people with whom you work, that it will spark conversation, enable connections to our faith, and empower leaders, parents, and middle-schoolers to live the life to which they are called—embracing love, acceptance, and compassion for all.

INTRODUCTION

Welcome to *These Are Our Bodies!*

These Are Our Bodies is a comprehensive faith and sexuality program for middle-schoolers that can be used in a variety of settings including Sunday morning classes, evening events, or seminars spanning a Friday afternoon and Saturday. The program is based on the universal needs of young people and their parents. In order to honor and lift up parents as the primary sexuality educators to their children, the program involves parents as an integral part of the program.

The program is a developmentally appropriate, creatively interactive, faith-based approach to sexuality that places human sexuality in the context of faith. Direct and indirect teaching around concepts such as God's creation, scripture, and sexuality as gift from God are intertwined throughout the sessions. Conversations and teaching around the stewardship of gifts, responsible behavior, and God's grace and love abound in this program.

Middle-schoolers need reassurance that their growth and development is normal and expected. As they continue their journey toward adulthood and independence, the church can provide the environment and opportunities to bridge the gap between their everyday lives and their faith lives. They need to know there is a place for them to ask their questions and receive honest answers. Adolescents respond to programs that give them new ways to look at their lives and the grace and space to explore their thoughts, feeling, and experiences. The sessions in *These Are Our Bodies Leader Guide* for Middle School explore concepts around our faith in ways that connect with young people and give them opportunities to strengthen their faith. The connection between our faith and sexuality is presented throughout the program through the modeling of the Facilitator and Small-Group Leaders, how questions are answered, and the atmosphere that is created.

These Are Our Bodies teaches that we are *all* God's children—loved and redeemed. Each of us is made in the image of God—good and holy. There is nothing that we can do to separate us from the love of God. Forgiveness and grace are gifts given to each of us and are born from God's love for us.

Human beings are made in the Image of God—perfectly made, but not perfect. Human beings are imperfect. We are best when we are open, vulnerable, and truthful with each other. These messages are embedded in the way that Facilitators and Small-Group Leaders answer questions and interact with the young people.

Components of These Are Our Bodies

Four intersecting and related resources make up *These Are Our Bodies* for Middle School:
> the *Foundation Book* (recommended for the Facilitator, for each Small-Group Leader, and for parents)
> the Middle-School *Leader Guide* (recommended for the Facilitator and each Small-Group Leader)
> the Middle-School *Parent Book* (recommended for each parent)
> the Middle-School *Participant Book* (recommended for each participant)

The *Leader Guide* uses and makes references to the *Foundation Book, Parent Book, and Participant Book*, all available through www.ChurchPublishing.org.

This *Leader Guide* is comprised of two sections. The Introduction you are reading now introduces the curriculum, describes parts of each lesson, focuses on recruitment and training of Small-Group Leaders, and provides information for Facilitators and Small-Group Leaders to implement the program. The second section has the plans for each of the 10 sessions in the program.

Leadership

To implement *These Are Our Bodies* a Facilitator and two or more Small-Group Leaders are needed.

FACILITATOR

The Facilitator will be the leader of each session, teaching the material and guiding the lesson. The Facilitators responsibilities include:
> preparing the room
> gathering the supplies
> making copies when needed
> teaching the session content in middle-school sessions
> teaching the session content in the parent sessions
> adjusting the length of sessions to conform to the amount of time allowed
> planning the sessions in light of the participants' needs
> giving participants the grace and space to learn on their own
> modeling self-awareness and comfort with their own sexuality
> calmly explaining issues around sexuality without relying on authoritative ways of interacting with middle-schoolers
> giving space to participants to explore their own ideas and beliefs without imposing their own ideas on others

SMALL-GROUP LEADERS

Small-Group Leaders provide the support to the participants and Facilitator during each session. Their responsibilities include:

> ➤ attending the small-group training
> ➤ working with other Small-Group Leaders to provide support to participants
> ➤ guiding participants in discussion and small-group activities
> ➤ being the eyes and ears of the Facilitator and alerting the Facilitator to any potential problems within the group
> ➤ giving participants the grace and space to learn on their own
> ➤ modeling self-awareness and ease with their own sexuality
> ➤ explaining calmly the issues around sexuality without relying on authoritative ways of interacting with participants
> ➤ giving space to participants to explore their own ideas and beliefs without imposing the Small-Group Leaders' ideas on others

Parts of Each Session

These Are Our Bodies has 10 sessions. Each session uses scripture as an integral piece of the program. As Episcopalians, we take the Bible seriously and seek to integrate the teaching of the Bible into our lives. The scripture used in *These Are Our Bodies* helps participants and parents deepen their connection between God, the Bible and sexuality. We have used the *Common English Bible* as our main translation. You will also see the *New International Version* and the *New Revised Standard Version* as well.

Below are the session titles and the scriptures referenced in each session:

> ➤ SESSION 1:   You are GOD'S CREATION (Genesis 1:1–31; Galatians 5:22–23)
> ➤ SESSION 2:   You are COMPLEX (Psalm 139: 13–14)
> ➤ SESSION 3:   You are ACCEPTED (Genesis 1:27)
> ➤ SESSION 4:   You are RELATIONAL (Part 1) (John 15:13; 1 Corinthians 13:4–7; 1 Samuel 18:1–5; 20:1–42)
> ➤ SESSION 5:   You are RELATIONAL (Part 2) (Ruth 1:8–17)
> ➤ SESSION 6:   You are RESPONSIBLE (Ephesians 4:1–3)
> ➤ SESSION 7:   You are KNOWLEDGEABLE (Proverbs 2:10–11)
> ➤ SESSION 8:   You are CONNECTED (1 Kings 19:11–12)
> ➤ SESSION 9:   You are EMPOWERED (Philippians 2:2–5)
> ➤ SESSION 10: You are THOUGHTFUL (Romans 12:2)

Each of the 10 sessions has five parts that work together to create a hands-on interactive approach to learning: GATHER, GAME, GRAPPLE, GUIDE, and GO. The parts offer creative and playful activities to engage the material and participants in ways that provide intentional group formation, time to wrestle with new material, words of blessing and affirmation, and time to move from the sessions back into the world. The Facilitator leads each session with the help of Small-Group Leaders who facilitate the games, activities, and discussions.

GATHER

In Holy Eucharist, we are called together using a collect. We are collected together for a common purpose. In each session's GATHER, the Facilitator, Small-Group Leaders, and participants come together for the common purpose of learning and being in community. Part of group life is the intentional coming together of the group and the establishment of norms. This is an acknowledgment and reminder that we are joining an intentional community—especially a covenant community—that is best served by common ground rules that shape our sessions. In each session, the Facilitator, Small-Group Leaders, and participants commit to common ground rules, called the HOPE[3] ground rules, which will be fully explained on pages 13–14 of this *Leader Guide*. As you will see, HOPE reminds us of the expectations of the community. The GATHER part of the session provides a prayerful way to bring participants together to form the group for the work ahead.

GATHER also gives participants and the Small-Group Leaders a way to transition from the distractions outside of the room to the group. GATHER is lead by the Facilitator in the beginning of the program and shifts leadership to the participants later in the program.

The last part of GATHER is the answering of the Question Box questions that were written by participants in the previous session. Directions and a process for answering those questions is discussed on page 14 of this *Leader Guide*.

GAME

After GATHER, the GAME provides both a learning tool for participants and an ice-breaker. In each session, the GAME makes connections and breaks down barriers between participants, the Facilitator, and Small-Group Leaders . . . and between participants themselves. Middle-schoolers learn easily when they are playing and moving their bodies. The GAME part of the session opens the opportunity for creative thinking and learning.

GRAPPLE

These Are Our Bodies introduces complex ideas and concepts through the GRAPPLE portion of the session. Learning to wrestle and wrangle with the content is critical to the learning process. Each GRAPPLE includes teaching by the Facilitator and discussions in either the large group as a whole or in small groups. GRAPPLE provides the environment and time for participants to further explore the concepts they are learning and apply those concepts to their lives of faith. Participants are invited to GRAPPLE with the content to accomplish the session objectives.

---

3 The authors have done their best, without success, to track down the original source of the HOPE acronym. No copyright infringement is intended. If notified, they will gladly credit the original author in future editions of *These Are Our Bodies*.

GUIDE

As a Christian community concerned with building up the body of Christ, the work of blessing and affirmation is key to our mission. The GUIDE part of the sessions addresses this need for blessing, affirmation, and empowerment of everyone in the group, including the Facilitator, Small-Group Leaders, and participants. The GUIDE helps participants practice using words of wisdom and encouragement to empower each other. As part of the GUIDE, participants are invited to write a question for the Question Box.[4]

GO

Our Episcopal liturgy sends the gathered community out into the world with a missive to empower faithful community. The GO part of the session is a sending forth ritual that guides the return to life outside of the sacred space of the session. The GO part will be lead by a Small-Group Leaders or the Facilitator.

HOPE Ground Rules

A big goal of *These Are Our Bodies* is the formation of a group that provides a safe place for participants to honestly and openly engages the content of the program. In the church, when we do our most important work, we often form what are called *covenant groups*. Covenant groups form to help their members deal with difficult topics and grow together.[5] The concept of covenant is a biblical one drawn from motifs in the Old Testament. In Genesis, we learn that God formed a covenant with Noah and set the rainbow in the sky as a reminder of that covenant. In Genesis, we also hear the call for the people to be God's people—a deep covenant relationship. In the Book of Common Prayer, the theme of covenant weaves throughout the *Celebration and Blessing of a Marriage*. Today, we see covenants as promises between people.

In this context of *These Are Our Bodies*, the covenants are between the Small-Group Leaders, the Facilitator, participants, and parents. We will go over each aspect of the HOPE[6] covenant:
> **H** stands for *honesty*. In *These Are Our Bodies*, honesty is important. Participants will have many questions, and the Facilitator and Small-Group Leaders promise to answer questions honestly. They will give participants the information they need in a way that they can understand. Participants will also promise to be honest about their questions and their feelings.

---

4 More detail about the role of the Question Box is found on pages 14–15 of this *Leader Guide*, as well as information for the Facilitator and the Small-Group Leaders for answering questions from the Question Box.

5 This theme of *covenant* not only informs our group ground rules for the program, it encompasses an overarching ethic of love, grace, and compassion at the foundation of the teaching and our lives as faithful people. As the program progresses, lean on theme to re-tell the story of God's grace in our lives and how that unearned love compels us to love others. In the words of Standing Commission on Liturgy and Music, "God's covenant of creating, redeeming, and sustaining love, shapes our lives as Christians in relation to God and to God's creation; this calls us to live with love compassion, justice and peace toward all creatures, friend or foe, neighbor or stranger." (p. 28, Supplemental Materials)

6 The authors have done their best, without success, to track down the original source of the HOPE acronym. No copyright infringement is intended. If notified, they will gladly credit the original author in future editions of *These Are Our Bodies*.

➤ **O** stands for *openness*. In *These Are Our Bodies*, being open is imperative for us to learn and grow. We want participants to be open to each other and their Small-Group Leaders. We want the group to use good listening skills to hear and respond to one another, both lovingly and respectfully. And we want to be open to the work of the Holy Spirit in and among us.

➤ **P** stands for *privacy*. Privacy is a core concept that enables participants to feel comfortable in sharing our ideas and feelings. We want to hear about the experiences of the participants, and we ask that if participants are telling about an experience that they leave the names out of the story, which will protect privacy. We also ask that people keep what the other participants say in this room. We do want the participants to share the good things that they are learning, but want them to leave the names out of their stories. The Facilitator promises not to tell the parents what individual participants say or do. *This piece is critical.* The Facilitator and Small-Group Leaders may tell the parents what the entire group did or summarize a discussion to share with the parents. The Facilitator and Small-Group Leaders will not tell parents the details of any one participant. One of the underlying commitments is to the safety of the children in our care. When working with children, leaders might wonder when the promise of confidentiality or privacy should be broken. The safety of the child or of other people trumps confidentiality. If you suspect that the child has been harmed, will be abused, will hurt themselves, or may cause harm to others, the leader should act immediately. Leaders have an obligation to report any suspected abuse or any suspicion that a child might hurt themselves or others. In the case of suspected abuse or potential harm to themselves or others, leaders will report their concerns to both the clergy at the church and Child Protective Services.[7] The Facilitator and the Small-Group Leaders will tell participants about this exception to the privacy and confidentiality rule.

➤ **E** stands for *enthusiasm*. We ask that everyone enter into this with a spirit of fun and wonder. To be enthusiastic comes from the root word *entheos* meaning to be inspired by God[8]. The spirit of God is in and amongst us. The story of creation, the gift of sexuality, and the blessings of relationships are also filled with wonder and are definitely something about which to be enthusiastic.

In the GATHER portion of the session, the litany will be a reminder of the HOPE ground rules and the promises that we have made to each other:

Honesty: We commit to sharing what we really think.

Openness: We commit to being open to what others say, both our group members and our leaders, and most of all to God.

Privacy: We commit to keeping what is said and done here within this space.

Enthusiasm: We commit to laughter, fun, and a sense of wonder.

The Role of the Question Box

The Question Box is an important part of *These Are Our Bodies* for Middle School. Participants are asked to write questions for the Facilitator and Small-Group Leaders to answer. Participants add questions to

---

7 The phone numbers for Child Protective Services can be found at https://www.childwelfare.gov/.

8 http://www.oxforddictionaries.com/us/definition/american_english/enthusiasm (*entheos,* "possessed by a god, inspired"; based on *theos,* "god").

the Question Box each week, and questions are answered by the Facilitator and Small-Group Leaders each week.

Every group of young people presents different questions. The Question Box is one way that *These Are Our Bodies* adapts to fit what the participants in each group are pondering and address their questions in a safe environment. Having each participant write a question empowers the group to dive into the material in a personal way. The participants invest more when you answer the questions and when they see their question is on the list.

The Facilitator will want to make a Question Box for the program. Cover a shoebox with bright paper and decorate with question marks, exclamation points, and doodles. Make the box fun. Keep pencils and scrap paper for the questions with the box. Having a different color paper for each round of questions (for each session) will help the Facilitator ensure that every participant writes a question for the Question Box.

The Facilitator and the Small-Group Leaders will gather to read and discuss the questions as a group. Participants are beginning to think about their own behavior and how these concepts play out in their lives. Small-Group Leaders will seek to answer their questions directly, ensuring that they include the three parts of a concise and accurate answer when possible: *knowledge, skill,* and a *faith connection*.

The Small-Group Leaders and the Facilitator will meet after each session to debrief the session and plan how to answer the questions written for the Question Box in that session. During the meeting with the Small-Group Leaders and the Facilitator, the Facilitator reads one question at a time and asks the Small-Group Leaders:
- What are the participants asking?
- What does a person this age need to know about this topic?

As mentioned, when the Facilitator and Small-Group Leaders answer questions, seek to include three things:
- knowledge
- skill(s)
- a faith connection

Let's explore each of these in more detail:

Knowledge:
Seek to give the most brief, yet accurate answer to the question. You will want to remember that you are a conveyor of knowledge. The answers to a young person's questions should be direct and free from loaded language. When discussing the way to answer questions, the Facilitator and Small-Group Leaders should assume good intent and seek to answer their question directly and honestly giving straightforward information and knowledge. Most leaders will find it necessary to simplify the answer or even wonder if a certain question should be answered. Even though the Facilitator or the Small-Group Leaders may be challenged by a certain question, we urge you to find a way to answer the question in a brief and trustful way.

The Facilitator and Small-Group Leader may want to ask themselves: Will a participant have to re-learn this material that we are teaching? If the answer is *yes*, look for an accurate way to address the questions. Remember that answering each and every question will build trust within the group; if the question is not answered in this program, participants will find out the answer another way that might not be a knowledgeable answer.

Skill:
The second part involves giving a skill that the participants will be able to use when they encounter this situation or word again. For example, when answering a question about a slang term that is derogatory, you could add this skill: "Although you may see that word written or used by your peers, as Christians we seek to respect all persons and using this word is disrespectful and hurtful to others. This word, *(provide an appropriate alternative)*, would be a better choice." Small-Group Leaders can also add how they might handle a similar situation or something that the young person might want to consider when faced with a similar decision.

Faith Connection:
The last piece adds a faith connection that links questions about our bodies and sexuality to our Christian life together. These are both implicit and explicit messages that (a) model to participants how our faith intersects with our sexuality and (b) lay a foundation for our lives of Christians. Our faith also informs and guides our choices, attitudes, and behaviors. Making these faith connections helps us to ask: "Where is God in this?"

In the following example, these three parts work together to give a direct, unemotional, but brief answer that includes layers of knowledge, a skill, and a faith connection to specific issues around sexuality. Here is an example: The question asked is "Do I have to have sex?"

> ➤ *Knowledge:* No, you do not have to have sexual intercourse or engage in sexual activity. No one should ever be forced to have sexual intercourse. Being sexually active is a personal decision that men and women make for themselves. No one should ever pressure you to do something that makes you feel uncomfortable or that you are not ready to do. You might think that sexual intercourse is something you never want to do. It is normal for people your age not to be interested in sexual things. Don't be surprised if your feelings about dating, marriage, and having children change as you get older.

> ➤ *Skill:* If you feel uncomfortable or if someone tries to make you do something you do not want to do, tell the person, "No," and be forceful. Tell an adult who has good ears for kids and teens. Doctors, nurses, teachers, counselors, and principals have special training to help keep children and teens safe. If one adult does not really listen to you, tell another adult. Most youth directors and ministers also have good ears for young people—they will know what to do to keep you safe. You might hear from a friend that they have been hurt by someone. If you find yourself in this situation, tell a principal or a teacher that your friend has been hurt. You will be helping your friend more than you will ever know!

> ➤ *Faith Connection:* Sexual intercourse is a gift from God—something that is beautiful, tender, and precious. We should never use our sexuality in a selfish or forceful way. It is good to do everything we can to keep ourselves and others safe.

The Facilitator and Small-Group Leaders together decide how to answer each question before you decide who will answer. The Facilitator makes notes on each question, jotting down which points need to be included in the answer. After the discussion about *how* to answer the question, ask *who* would like to answer that question at the beginning of the next session. When you are deciding who will answer the questions, think about ways to have different people answer similar questions. If you have three questions on shaving, for example, have different Small-Group Leaders answer each of those questions. You could have a different aspect of the questions answered each time.

Make sure every question is answered—even if questions are *very* similar. Honoring the questions is vital to creating the open and welcoming space. When Small-Group Leaders answer questions about the opposite gender, they also model that both men and women can answer these questions and learn that they can go to their parents or trusted adult for answers, no matter their gender.

Once all of the questions are read and a Small-Group Leader has volunteered to answer each question, ask a Small-Group Leader to write the questions on the easel paper. The questions can be re-worded if they are confusing; correct spelling errors as needed.

Introducing *These Are Our Bodies* to your Church

Developing *These Are Our Bodies* in your church involves:
- facilitation and planning
- promotion
- budget, invitation, and registration
- planning for supplies and snacks
- recruiting Small-Group Leaders
- training leaders

Each of the aspects are addressed in detail below:

FACILITATION AND PLANNING

The 10 sessions in this curriculum are flexible in design to meet the needs of youth groups, Sunday School, and Retreats. There are three types of sessions: parent-only sessions, participant-only sessions and a joint participant-and-parent session. As you think about ways to use this curriculum, you will want to include each of those types of sessions.

Option 1: 10 Weekly Sessions

One way to use this curriculum is to plan ten 70–90 minute sessions with participants. You could carve out time on Sunday morning and extend the session time to include breakfast or lunch.

Training of the Small-Group Leader	90 minutes
Pre-Session for Parents	90 minutes

Sessions 1–7	70–90 minutes
Session 8	120 minutes (participant-and-parent session)
Sessions 9–10	70–90 minutes

With this model, parents have time to understand the program and to be an integral part of *These Are Our Bodies*. Session 8 gives parents time to experience what the participants are learning and to practice the skills that they are learning around answering participants' questions.

Option 2: Retreat

A retreat gives the group time to explore the curriculum without the constraints of a Sunday morning or a weekday evening. Often participants bond over an entire weekend in ways that never happen in shorter time spans. The experience of "going away" for the weekend helps break down barriers that exist because of preconceived notions about certain spaces and times.

Consider what a retreat center offers that would add to the experience. Often the staff of a camp and retreat center are eager to help by working with the goals for the weekend. For example, if a retreat center offers a low-ropes challenge course, use the processing time after a course to tie in specific elements of the curriculum. Also consider utilizing natural school breaks like summer and three-day weekends.

Pre-Session for Small-Group Leaders	90 minutes (prior to the retreat)
Pre-Session for Parents	90 minutes (prior to the retreat)

Day 1:

Session 1	90 minutes in the afternoon
Dinner	
Session 2	90 minutes in the evening

Day 2:

Breakfast	
Session 3	90 minutes in the morning
Break	
Sessions 4 and 5	150 minutes in the morning
Lunch and Break	
Session 6	90 minutes in the afternoon
Dinner	
Session 7	90 minutes in the evening

Day 3:

Breakfast	
Session 9 and Session 10	90 minutes after breakfast
Session 8 (with parents)	90 minutes

Option 3: Youth Group

Youth ministry is already designed for cultivating relationships between young people and trusted adults. Though *These Are Our Bodies* encourages more of the same, be sure to evaluate whether the existing youth leaders should also be the Small-Group Leaders in this program.

No matter what day of the week or amount of time your youth group meets, this program can flow easily into existing structures. As with any youth group, incorporating food into the sessions is a great way to take a short break or to begin. The GRAPPLE portions of the sessions are the longest but can be broken up with a short snack time or meal.

The first session will take the most time because it introduces so many of the components.

A typical session is broken down as follows:

GATHER	20 minutes
GAME	20 minutes
GRAPPLE	45 minutes
GUIDE	15 minutes
GO	5 minutes
TOTAL	**105 minutes**

There is no greater time challenge than transitions. Young people are known for moving at their own pace. Having a timer on hand or another visual signal is helpful. Reminders to watch time are written within the sessions, but it is always a good idea to appoint one Small-Group Leader the keeper of the clock. By delegating this task, your attention can remain on the content and participants.

PROMOTION

Announcements in the church newsletter or on the church website will give families the opportunity to put this program and the specific dates on their calendars. Planning a date several months in advance gives families time to plan around the program, enabling more families to participate.

BUDGETING, INVITATION, AND REGISTRATION

Part of the planning process is determining the expenses of the program and whether (and how much) you will charge for the program. As you put together the budget, make sure to include:

- ➤ *Leader Guides* and *Foundation Books* for the Facilitator and all Small-Group Leaders
- ➤ *Parent Books* and *Foundation Books* for parents
- ➤ *Participant Books* for participants
- ➤ snacks and meals

> ➤ supplies: easel paper, markers, pens, pencils, paper, small white boards, colored scrap paper
> ➤ additional supplies unique to each session (See the Supplies list at the beginning of each session.)

You will want to send out a letter to families that describes *These Are Our Bodies* (a sample letter is below) and a registration form (a sample registration form is also below).

Sample These Are Our Bodies Registration Form

For Grades XX-XX
Dates: *(insert overall dates and times of the program)*
Schedule: *(insert more detailed schedule, being sure to include the parents' session)*

Very Important: Parents and participants should plan to attend all of their sessions!

Participant Name:

Address:

Birth date: Grade: Sex:

Parent Phone Number(s):

Name(s) of Parent(s) or Guardian:

Parent(s) E-mail Address:

Name(s) of Siblings and Their Ages:

Please tell us about your child on the back of this form. Mention anything that will help us in working with him or her.

Registration is due: *(insert deadline).* Please register early so that we may accommodate as many participants as possible!

A fee of *(insert fee if applicable)* to cover cost of supplies is due with this registration.
- No phone registrations, please.
- Please make your check payable to: *(insert name of church).*
- Please mail to: *(insert address of the church).*

Sample Family Letter

Dear Family,

Our church is offering *These Are Our Bodies* to our middle-school children. It is a program developed by Church Publishing Incorporated that is based on the needs of both middle-schoolers and their parents. To honor and lift up parents as the primary sexuality educators to their children, the program involves parents as an integral part of the program.

The program is a developmentally appropriate, creatively interactive, faith-based approach to sexuality that places human sexuality in the context of faith. Direct and indirect teaching around concepts such as God's creation, scripture, and sexuality as gift from God are intertwined throughout the sessions. Conversations and teaching around the stewardship of gifts, responsible behavior, and God's grace and love abound in this program.

Topics of discussion include:
For Participants:
> Made in the Image of God
> Self-Image and Media
> Love
> Friendship and Infatuation
> Biological Sex, Gender Identity, Gender Expression, Romantic Attraction, and Sexual Attraction
> Sex as Fire
> Biblical Models of Friendship
> Refusal Skills
> Prostitution and Pornography
> Cyber Bullying
> Sexually Transmitted Infections
> Birth Control
> Assertive and Aggressive Behavior
> Facts and Myths around Sexuality
> Decision-Making
> Listening Skills
> Value Clarification

For Parents:
> Understanding Sexuality
> Scripture and Parenting
> How to Answer Your Child's Questions
> How to Listen

The Schedule for the Sessions: (insert schedule)

How to Register: (describe how you will accept registrations)

PLANNING FOR SUPPLIES AND SNACKS

Each lesson gives a list of supplies that you will need for that session. You might want to gather scissors, pencils, Post-it Notes®, sticky easel pads, and markers to keep on hand. Additional supplies unique to each session will be found in the Supplies list at the start of every session.

Plan ahead to order *These Are Our Bodies* materials for the Facilitator, Small-Group Leaders, parents or guardians, and participants. Order the books at least three weeks before your Small-Group Training. You will need to order:

➤ *Leader Guides* and *Foundation Books* for the Facilitator and all Small-Group Leaders
➤ *Parent Books* and *Foundation Books* for parents
➤ *Participant Books* for participants

Providing drinks and snacks is also an essential part of the program. The participants and adults can be nervous or anxious when discussing sexuality. Snacks and drinks give middle-schoolers a reason to get up and move around the room, if they need it. Munching on baby carrots or chips can help release some of the tension and anxiety. When the Facilitator introduces the HOPE ground rules of the program to the participants in Session 1, talk briefly about the open concept of getting snacks. The participants can help themselves as long as the Facilitator doesn't notice them. *In other words, don't go as a group.* The concept of self-regulation with the participants in terms of when they might need a snack, drink, or to go to the bathroom is an integral part of creating a safe space where middle-schoolers will feel comfortable asking questions.

RECRUITING SMALL-GROUP LEADERS

You will want a diverse group of Small-Group Leaders to model different ways of being faithful people in the church and world. At a minimum, make sure you have both male and female Small-Group Leaders as well as diversity in partnered status. You would want to include a variety of Small-Group Leaders in terms of race, culture, and orientation. Are the people you are thinking about partnered, married, divorced, remarried, widowed, or single? Although you may not have a broad range of Small-Group Leaders (you probably only need 4–6 Small-Group Leaders), being aware of diversity will be enable your program to be inclusive. Remember to observe safe church practices when considering whom to ask.

You will want at least two male and two female Small-Group Leaders for every 10 participants. When you break the groups up for small-group activities and discussions, assign both a male and female to each group. In addition to both male and female Small-Group Leaders, avoid selecting parents of middle-schoolers who are participating in the program.

Small-Group Leaders play an integral part in the program. Choose the leaders carefully to ensure a quality program. Some Facilitators look for nursing or medical professionals. Others look for counselors. With Small-Group Leaders, their occupation or experience in a special field is less important than the way Small-Group Leaders interact with kids and the gifts they bring by way of their interpersonal skills. If a Small-Group Leader is a professional who brings some expertise, it is best if they are able to let the lessons flow and will resist the temptation to hijack the process.

If possible, look for adults whom you have seen work with middle-schoolers. Ask yourself these questions:

➤ Will they able to lead participants by giving them grace and space to be comfortable and to learn on their own?
➤ Are they self-aware and comfortable with their own sexuality?

➤ Will they be able to calmly explain issues around sexuality without relying on authoritative ways of interacting with participants?

➤ Are they interested in helping participants learn and grow rather imposing their beliefs on the middle-schoolers?

Pre-Session Training of the Small-Group Leaders

 (90–120 Minutes)

Small-Group Leaders are essential to the success of the *These Are Our Bodies*. Before the program begins, set aside 1½–2 hours to train leaders. Invite the Small-Group Leaders to a training about one week before the sessions begin.

GOALS

➤ Small-Group Leaders will meet each other and get to know each other better.

➤ Facilitator will begin to establish a relationship with the Small-Group Leaders.

➤ Small-Group Leaders will become familiar with the goals of *These Are Our Bodies*.

➤ Facilitator will review the program.

➤ Facilitator will review the role of the Small-Group Leaders.

➤ Facilitator will address any questions or concerns.

SUPPLIES

➤ 1 *Foundation Book*, 1 *Leader Guide*, 1 *Participant Book*, and 1 *Parent Book* for each Small-Group Leader (For this pre-session, use the *Participant Books* and *Parent Books* that will be distributed to participants and parents next week.)

➤ copies of the schedule, 1 per Small-Group Leader

PREPARATION

➤ Have the four books for the Small-Group Leaders nearby.

➤ Have copies of the schedule nearby.

THE SESSION

Welcome Small-Group Leaders and say:

• Thank you for your willingness to be part of this program and to work closely with our middle-schoolers.

- Let's begin with a prayer for the young people in our care:
  Facilitator: The Lord be with you
  Small-Group Leaders: And also with you.
  Facilitator: Let us pray.

  God our Father, you see your children growing up in an unsteady and confusing world: Show them that your ways give more life than the ways of the world, and that following you is better than chasing after selfish goals. Help them to take failure, not as a measure of their worth, but as a chance for a new start. Give them strength to hold their faith in you, and to keep alive their joy in your creation; through Jesus Christ our Lord. *Amen.*[9]

Continue:

- Introduce yourself by name, then tell us how you came to be involved with *These Are Our Bodies*.

After the introductions, say:

- Thank you for introducing yourselves.
- Now that we know how each of you came to be involved with this program, let me spend a few minutes telling you how our church came to offer *These Are Our Bodies*.

Why These Are Our Bodies?

Explain why your church family values such conversations about sexuality and faith. If necessary, you could adapt these points:

- For several years we have been hearing from parents their desire for a program within the church that address the connection between faith and sexuality.
- As a church family, it is important that we step into these conversations with each other.
- Our church wants to empower parents to be the primary sexuality educators of their children.

Say:

- Before we go into the goals of the program, let's think about the parents and participants that we will be working with in *These Are Our Bodies*.
- What do parents of middle-schoolers need? What are their concerns? their apprehensions?
- How can we give parents the grace and space they need to receive the information and experience of this program?

Parents need information about young people at this stage of their lives. They also need to be equipped to answer their child's questions. Parents need a refresher on the developmental needs of their middle-schooler, and they need to know they are not alone—there is a community of faithful people helping them on this journey.

Continue:

- What do middle-schoolers need from a sexuality program?

Middle-schoolers need a safe place to ask questions, to learn new things, to explore their thoughts and feelings, and to spend time with adults (leaders and parents) who are willing to talk with them

9 Book of Common Prayer, page 829.

about what matters the most. Middle-schoolers also need knowledge, skills, and faith connections to navigate the next few years.

Our Goals
Say:

- *These Are Our Bodies* offers three main goals:
  - to lay the faith foundation for healthy sexuality
  - to give middle-schoolers the experiences and opportunities to explore sexuality in the context of their faith
  - to empower parents as the primary sexuality educators of their middle-schoolers
- Let's look at these more closely.
- *The first goal is to lay the faith foundation for healthy sexuality.*
  - *These Are Our Bodies* aims to go far beyond just a basic sharing of information about sex. We demonstrate to participants that their faith community is a trustworthy place to grow and mature and learn about the faith connection between their developing sexuality and God.
  - The program teaches that we are all God's children—loved and redeemed. Each of us is made in the image of God—good and holy. There is nothing that we can do to separate us from the love of God. Forgiveness and grace are gifts given to each of us and are born from God's love for us. Human beings are imperfect. We are best when we are open, vulnerable, and truthful with each other. These messages are embedded in the way that Facilitator and Small-Group Leaders answer questions and interact with the young people.
  - As participants continue their journey toward adulthood and independence, the church can provide the environment and opportunities to bridge the gap between their everyday lives and their faith lives. We will use prayer and scripture to discuss themes around sexuality.
  - Direct and indirect teaching around God's creation, scripture, and sexuality as gift from God are intertwined throughout the sessions. Conversations and teaching around the creation, responsible behavior, and God's grace and love abound in this program.
- *The second goal is to give participants the experiences and opportunities to explore sexuality in the context of their faith.*
  - The sessions in *These Are Our Bodies* are designed to teach concepts around our faith in ways that connect with young people and give them opportunities to go deeper in their faith. Each participant will receive a *Participant Book* that will guide them to reflect on what they are learning and make faith connections.
  - As topics around sexuality are introduced, taught, and discussed, we will continually connect that new knowledge with skills they can use in their everyday lives. The discussions and questions that we answer will make a concrete connection to our faith.
  - The program is a developmentally appropriate, creatively interactive, faith-based approach to sexuality that places human sexuality in the context of faith. Adolescents respond to programs that give them new ways to look at their lives along with the grace and space to explore their thoughts, feeling, and experiences. Middle-schoolers will receive reassurance that their growth and development is normal and expected. They need to know there is a place for them to ask their questions and receive honest answers.
  - Topics Include: Made in the Image of God, Self Image and Media, Love, Friendship and Infatuations, Biological Sex, Gender Identity, Gender Expression, Romantic Attraction, and Sexual Attraction, Sex as Fire, Biblical Models of Friendship, Refusal Skills, Prostitution

and Pornography, Cyber bullying, Sexually Transmitted Infections, Birth Control, Anatomy, Assertive and Aggressive Behavior, Facts and Fiction around Sexuality, Decision-Making, Anatomy, Listening Skills, Value Clarification, and Faith Connection.

- *The third goal is to empower parents as the primary sexuality educators of their middle-schoolers.*
  - ○ The best way to help families make the connection between faith and sexuality is by inviting participants and parents to learn and share at church. As a parent, it can be challenging to address issues around puberty, development, and sexuality. The issues young people face and the questions they have are biological, social, spiritual, cognitive, and emotional. The joint session with participants and parents (Session 8) gives families the time and space to explore a range of issues together.
  - ○ To help empower parents as the primary educators of their children, our Facilitator shares age-appropriate information and encourages participants to ask their parents questions and enter into conversations with them about the thoughts, feelings, and questions with which they wrestle. We recognize that there can be a wide range of beliefs and opinions about some controversial topics even at church, and we seek to empower all parents to effectively teach their children about faith and sexuality.
  - ○ A portion of the parent program is devoted to helping parents clarify values and communicate those values to their children in the form of a faith connection, as they answer questions about difficult or sensitive topics.

HOPE

Share with Small-Group Leaders the information on covenants and the HOPE ground rules found on pages 13–14 and 35–36. If Small-Group Leaders are experienced in ministry, this conversation can be brief. Feel free to adjust the time to allow for more discussion if Small-Group Leaders have not had much training in working with young people.

Invite and discuss questions or concerns.

Conclude the HOPE discussion:
- In the GATHER portion of every session, the HOPE litany will be a reminder of our ground rules and the promises that we have made to each other:

  Honesty: We commit to sharing what we really think.
  Openness: We commit to being open to what others say, both our group members and our leaders, and most of all to God.
  Privacy: We commit to keeping what is said and done here within this space.
  Enthusiasm: We commit to laughter, fun, and a sense of wonder.

The Role of the Small-Group Leader

Lead the group in a discussion of the role of Small-Group Leaders. Have Small-Group Leaders turn to page 26 in their *Leader Guide* (this page) to follow along as you discuss the points below.

Invite Small-Group Leaders to take turns reading each point. Note that each point ends with a question. Use these questions as conversation-starters, welcoming additional discussion:

- The primary role of the Small-Group Leader is to encourage and be supportive of participants. Learn the names of the participants in your group and let the Facilitator know about any concerns that you may have. Look for how the participants are doing: Are they comfortable? participating? engaged? *Question:* How do you feel about these suggestions?

- Silence does not mean non-participation. Sometimes, because of the subject, the only response young people will make is to listen. If they are listening actively, they will get a great benefit from the sessions. *Question:* Who has seen this in small groups before?

- Stay on the same level. Communication is encouraged by keeping the group in a circle facing each other and on the same level (all in chairs or all on the floor). Normally chairs are noisy when participants fidget in them. Having participants on the floor helps them to be comfortable and eliminates the distractions that chairs create! *Question:* Are you okay with joining participants on the floor?

- Participants will rarely ask personal questions of their Small-Group Leaders. One way to handle personal questions is to say, "What happened with me may not be accurate for everyone." "Let's see what is true for most people." The questions can then be answered in a large group. Or, "Remember our covenant of HOPE? This is an area that I need to keep private. I can answer that from a variety of perspectives." *Question:* How comfortable are you in responding this way?

- Assuming good intent is especially critical to our interaction with young people around sexuality. Although some of their questions to us could be interpreted as disrespectful or prodding, as Small-Group Leaders, when we assume the best intentions from participants, we engage them in an authentic way. We choose to make this about their growth and learning and not about ourselves. Assuming good intent and answering their questions with discernment and care ensures that you will not say something that is shaming to them. Shaming participants—or anyone for that matter—runs counter to our desire to build healthy relationships and a safe environment. Shame occurs when children hear that they are bad for things that they are thinking of, feeling, or doing. *Questions:* How do you feel about this suggestion? When have *you* experienced shaming around the issue of sexuality?

- There are no wrong answers! One of our goals is to help all participants feel comfortable in the sessions. One of the best ways to gain participants' trust is by welcoming all of their contributions. Don't look for "right" answers; look for participation. Accept whatever is offered and use it as a stepping-stone for discussion. See in their responses every "teachable moment" they offer and build on them. *Questions:* In what ways can you respond that let participants know their insights and responses are welcomed and respected?

- Ask for volunteers instead of calling on someone to answer or to read. Part of giving participants the space they need to absorb this information is allowing them to answer questions, offer comments, and read *when they feel ready*. Be aware that some middle-schoolers may not read well. Vocabulary terms and words that are new and unfamiliar add to their need for support as they read. Embarrassing a participant by telling them to read aloud can cause them to withdraw rather than engage. In these discussions about sexuality, participants will be anxious already. Seek to reduce their stress. *Question:* How could these suggestions help with the program?

- Many adults worry about behavior management in working with middle-schoolers. Presenting the material in an engaging way, with developmentally-appropriate material and pace, minimizes behavior challenges. If a participant is disturbing other participants, a Small-Group Leader may want to sit on the floor next to that individual. This is called *proximity* and is a great strategy. Normally, sitting near the participant or spreading participants out is all that is required. Proximity may also mean putting space between participants who might distract one another. *Question:* When have you seen this simple technique used? How did it help?

- Another typical coping behavior during sexuality conversations is giggling. Laughter and silliness can ripple through the group; you may feel you may have lost control. If this happens, try having everyone stand, move around, and then sit down again. You can also think of quick repeat-after-me statements, either serious or lighthearted, for example: "I am accepted by God" (serious); "God made all of us" (serious); "I collect toe jam" (lighthearted); "My armpits smell like roses" (lighthearted). Breaking up the seating arrangement and introducing movement can also help shift the tone. Giggling and laughing usually indicate embarrassment. Having both males and females in a group actually helps to lessen the laughter and giggles. Watch to see if one person is beginning the laughter interruptions, then have a Small-Group Leader sit next to that participant. *Question:* When have you seen giggling or laughing interfere with a group's interaction?

Say:
- Now that we have gone over a few practical suggestions for Small-Group Leaders, let's look at the program and go over Session 1 together.
- *These Are Our Bodies* includes 2 pre-sessions and 10 regular sessions. The first pre-session is this training for the Small-Group Leaders. The second pre-session is a preview session for parents. The next 10 sessions are for the participants; note that Session 8 includes both participants and their parents.
- This is the schedule of our program.

Distribute copies of the schedule and briefly review the titles of the lessons. If you are using *These Are Our Bodies* over 10 weeks, propose meeting after each session to review the session and plan for the next session. (Instructions for this weekly "debriefing" are included at the end of every session.) If you are using a retreat format, review the retreat schedule; remember that you will want to review how things are going with the Small-Group Leaders throughout the retreat. "Checking in" between the Small-Group Leaders and the Facilitator is vital to the success of the overall program. Emphasize to leaders that withholding information about a particular concern may create more challenges in the future.

Say:
Let's review the curriculum.
- *These Are Our Bodies for Middle School* is formed of four intersecting and related resources designed for use within the church—the *Foundation Book*, the middle-school *Leader Guide*, the middle-school *Parent Book*, and the middle-school *Participant Book*. The *Leader Guide* uses and makes references to the *Foundation Book*, *Parent Book,* and *Participant Book*.
- Small-Group Leaders each have a copy of the *Foundation Book* and the *Leader Guide*.
- Each participant will have a copy of the *Participant Book*.
- Parents will have copies of the *Parent Book* and will be encouraged to also have and read the *Foundation Book*.

Distribute to Small-Group Leaders their *Foundation Books* and *Leader Guides*. Explain:

- Let's turn to Session 1 on page 41 of the *Leader Guide*.
- Each of the 10 sessions has five parts that work together to create a hands-on interactive approach to learning: GATHER, GAME, GRAPPLE, GUIDE, and GO. The session parts offer creative and playful ways to engage with the material and participants in ways that provide intentional group formation, engage the nature of middle-schoolers, offer time to wrestle with new material, provide words of blessing and affirmation, and allow time to move from the sessions back into the world. The Facilitator leads each session with the help of Small-Group Leaders who facilitate the games, activities, and discussions.
- *Let's look at the GATHER part of the sessions:* In our Holy Eucharist, we are called together using a collect. We are "collected" together for a common purpose. During GATHER, the Facilitator, leaders, and participants are gathered together for the common purpose of learning together and being in community. Part of group life is the intentional coming together of the group and the establishment of norms. Part of this work is an acknowledgment and reminder that we are joining an intentional community—a covenant community that is best served with some common ground rules that will shape our time together. Each session, the Facilitator, Small-Group Leaders, and participants commit to common ground rules by saying the HOPE ground rules Litany, reminding each other of the expectations of the community. The GATHER part of the session sets aside an intentional and prayerful way to bring the participants together to form a group for the work ahead of them. GATHER also gives participants and Small-Group Leaders a way to transition from the distractions outside of the room and focus on the group. GATHER will be led by a Small-Group Leader for the first two sessions, then shift to volunteer participants in remaining sessions. The last part of GATHER includes answering questions from the Question Box that were written in the previous sessions.
- *Let's look at the GAME part:* After GATHER, the GAME offers both a learning tool for participants and an icebreaker. In each session, the GAME is a fun way to make connections and break down barriers both between participants, Facilitator, and Small-Group Leaders and between the participants themselves. Middle-schoolers learn easily when they are playing games and moving their bodies. The GAME provides creative thinking, learning, movement, and more than a little fun to the program.
- *Let's look at the GRAPPLE part: These Are Our Bodies* introduces new and complex ideas and concepts. Learning to wrestling and wrangle with the content is critical to the learning process. GRAPPLE includes teaching by the Facilitator and discussion in either the large group or in small-group sessions. GRAPPLE provides environment and time for participants to struggle with understanding new concepts, applying them to their lives.
- *Let's look at the GUIDE part:* As a Christian community concerned with building up the body of Christ, the work of blessing and affirmation is key to our mission. GUIDE addresses this need for blessing, affirmation, and empowerment of everyone in the group, including the Facilitator, Small-Group Leaders, and participants. GUIDE provides words of wisdom and encouragement offered by Small-Group Leaders to participants *and* by participants to each other and their Small-Group Leaders. As part of each GUIDE, participants write questions for the Question Box.
- *Let's look at the GO part:* Our Episcopal Liturgy sends the gathered community out into the world with a missive to empower faithful community. The GO portion of the session includes

a sending-forth ritual that makes it possible to return to life outside of the sacred space of the session. GO will be lead by a Small-Group Leader for the first two sessions.

- Unless other arrangements are made, the Facilitator gathers the material and guides the sessions.

Answering Participants' Questions

Show Small-Groups Leaders the Question Box. Continue:

- Let's talk about how we want to answer in the sessions, not only questions from the Question Box, but any other questions that may come up.
- The Question Box will be used each session. At the end of each session, participants write questions for the Question Box. We will gather those questions, and, after participants leave, we (as leaders) will talk about each question and decide how we want to answer the question.
- The two questions we will ask ourselves are:
  - What is the participant asking?
  - What do they need to know?
- Every group of young people presents different questions. The Question Box is one way in which *These Are Our Bodies* adapts to fit what participants in each group are pondering in a safe environment. Having each participant write a question empowers the group to dive into the material in a personal way. Participants invest more when you answer the questions and when they see their questions are on the list.
- The Facilitator guides participants to write a question for the Question Box, by saying:
  - At different times you will have the opportunity to write questions for the box. I want to invite you to think about questions you might already have. Maybe you have a joke you don't understand or a word you don't understand. Maybe your friend asked you a question and you want to submit it. I will give you an honest answer. Everyone will write a question for the Question Box. You will have an opportunity to ask a question for the Question Box at the end of each session.
- *These Are Our Bodies* teaches that we are all God's children—loved and redeemed. Each of us is made in the image of God—good and holy. There is nothing that we can do to separate us from the love of God. Forgiveness and grace are gifts given to each of us and are born from God's love for us. Human beings are imperfect. We are best when we are open, vulnerable, and truthful with each other. These messages are embedded in the way that Facilitators and Small-Group Leaders answer questions and interact with the young people.
- When you as Small-Group Leader answer questions, seek to include three things: *knowledge*, a *skill,* and a *faith connection*. See pages 15–17 for more information about including these three components in an answer to a question.
- The answers to a young person's questions should be direct and free from loaded language. When we hear questions, the Facilitator and Small-Group Leaders assume good intent and seek to answer their question directly and honestly. If you can't answer the question and need to research the answer or discern a good way to answer the question, honestly acknowledge that you need time to answer the question well. The second piece adds an applicable skill to the answer.

- Small-Group Leaders can potentially add how they might handle a similar situation or something that the young person might want to consider when faced with a similar decision. The third piece adds a faith connection that links questions about our bodies and sexuality to our Christian life together.
- Let's look at an example.

Together turn to this page in the *Leader Guide* (if they haven't been following along to this point). Say:
- In the following example the three parts work together to give a direct, unemotional, but brief answer that has layers of *knowledge*, *skill*, and a *faith connection* to specific issues around sexuality.
- This is the question: Do I have to have sex?
- Let's ask ourselves the two questions that come first.
  - What is the participant asking? *(Pause for discussion.)*
  - What do they need to know? *(Pause for discussion.)*

Invite volunteers to read these answers aloud as the group follows along:
- *Knowledge:* No, you do not have to have sexual intercourse or engage in sexual activity. No one should ever be forced to have sexual intercourse. Being sexually active is a personal decision that men and women make for themselves. No one should ever pressure you to do something that makes you feel uncomfortable or that you are not ready to do. You might think that sexual intercourse is something you never want to do. It is normal for girls and boys your age not to be interested in sexual things. Don't be surprised if your feelings about dating, marriage, and having children change as you get older.
- *Skill:* If you feel uncomfortable or someone tries to make you do something you do not want to do—tell the person "No," and be forceful. Tell an adult who has good ears for kids and teens. Doctors, nurses, teachers, counselors, and principals have special training to help keep children and teens safe. If one adult does not really listen to you, tell another adult. Most youth directors and ministers also have good ears for young people—they will know what to do to keep you safe. You might hear from a friend that they have been hurt by someone else. If you find yourself in this situation, tell a principal or a teacher that your friend has been hurt. You will be helping your friend more than you will ever know!
- *Faith Connection:* Sexual intercourse is a gift from God—something that is beautiful, tender, and precious. We should never use our sexuality in a selfish or forceful way. It is good to do everything we can to keep ourselves and others safe.

Continue the discussion:
- What surprised you about those answers?
- Remember that I will be in the sessions and can help answer any questions that come up.
- What other questions or reflections do you have?

Conclude the session:
- Thank you for your enthusiasm and your willingness to do this very important work.
- Let's close with Prayer.

Facilitator: The Lord be with you.
Small-Group Leaders: And also with you.
Facilitator: Let us pray.

Facilitator: Loving and gracious God, creator and sustainer of all,
All: who knows the challenges and joys of adolescence,
Facilitator: who made us in the image of the God and calls us "very good,"
All: who gives us a ministry that demand our best efforts,
Facilitator: whose presence fills us with gladness,
All: we thank you for the leaders gathered here,
Facilitator: for their generous hearts,
All: for their abundant gifts,
Facilitator: for their willingness to walk on this journey.
All: We thank you for giving us this empowering work.
Facilitator: We confess that we may be nervous or anxious.
All: We acknowledge our tendency to control.
Facilitator: Bless us with calm spirits born of your *love.*
All: Bless us with unburdened hearts to listen.
Facilitator: Bless us with patience, humor, and joy.
All: And keep us ever mindful of your love and grace. *Amen.*

Preview Session for Parents

 (90 minutes)

GOALS

> Provide parents an overview of *These Are Our Bodies.*
> Go over the goals of the program.
> Introduce the HOPE ground rules.
> Review the curriculum.
> Review the role of parents as the primary sexuality educators of their children.
> Teach a way to answer middle-schoolers' questions.

SUPPLIES

> pencils or pens (1 per participant)
> *These Are Our Bodies Parent Books* (1 per parent)
> *These Are Our Bodies Foundation Books* (1 per parent or parent couple)
> HOPE poster (Download from the *These Are Our Bodies* Middle-School Leader Guide page: https://www.churchpublishing.org/theseareourbodiesmsleader.)
> easel and easel paper

> ➤ markers (2 or 3)
> ➤ nametags (1 per parent and Small-Group Leader)

PREPARATION

> ➤ Set up room in a U shape with chairs.
> ➤ Place easel at the front of the U.
> ➤ Have *Parent Books* and *Foundation Books* by the Facilitator's chair.
> ➤ Seat Small-Group Leaders throughout the U, not together.

THE SESSION

Say:
- Thank you for coming to the introduction session for *These Are Our Bodies*.
- We hope to do a few things in our time together.
- We are going to:
  - review the goals of the program
  - introduce the topics that will be covered
  - talk about the schedule
  - introduce a model for answering participants' questions about sexuality and faith
- And we promise that we will adjourn by *(insert time)* to get you home to your families.
- I am *(insert name)*, the Facilitator of the program. I will be leading with the help of *(insert names of Small-Group Leaders)*, our Small-Group Leaders.
- Let's begin with prayer.

> *Facilitator:* The Lord be with you.
> *Small-Group Leaders*: And also with you.
> *Facilitator:* Let us pray.
>
> Almighty God, giver of life and love, bless these parents. Grant
> them wisdom and devotion in the ordering of their common
> life, that each may be to the other a strength in need, a
> counselor in perplexity, a comfort in sorrow, and a companion
> in joy. And so knit their wills together in your will and their
> spirits in your Spirit, that they may live together in love and
> peace all the days of their lives; through Jesus Christ our Lord.
> *Amen.*[10]

Continue:
- Let's start with introductions.
- Please introduce yourself, tell us how you came to be in this session, and one thing you hope to gain from today's time together.

---

10 adapted from Book of Common Prayer, page 844.

When introductions have concluded, say:
- There are three goals for *These Are Our Bodies*:
  ○ to lay the faith foundation for sexuality
  ○ to give participants the experiences and opportunities to explore sexuality in the context of their faith
  ○ to empower parents as the primary sexuality educators of their children, no matter their age
  ○ Let's explore each one of those goals individually.
- The first goal is to lay the faith foundation for sexuality:
  ○ *These Are Our Bodies* aims to go far beyond just a basic sharing of information about sex. To address the first goal, *These Are Our Bodies*, builds the faith foundation for participants that their faith community is a trustworthy place to grow and mature and learn about the faith connection between their developing sexuality and God.
  ○ The program teaches that we are all God's children—loved and redeemed. Each of us is made in the image of God—good and holy. There is nothing that we can do to separate us from the love of God. Forgiveness and grace are gifts given to each of us and are born from God's love for us. Human beings are imperfect. We are best when we are open, vulnerable, and truthful with each other. These messages are embedded in the way that Facilitators and Small-Group Leaders answer questions and interact with the young people.
  ○ As participants continue their journey toward adulthood and independence, the church can provide the environment and opportunities to bridge the gap between their everyday lives and their faith lives. We will use prayer and scripture to discuss themes around sexuality.
  ○ Direct and indirect teaching around God's creation, scripture, and sexuality as gift from God are intertwined throughout the sessions. Conversations and teaching around the creation, responsible behavior, and God's grace and love abound in this program.
- The second goal is to give participants the experiences and opportunities to explore sexuality in the context of their faith:
  ○ In meeting the second goal, the sessions in *These Are Our Bodies* are designed to teach concepts around our faith in ways that connect with young people and give them opportunities to go deeper in their faith. Each participant receives a *Participant Book* that guides them to reflect on what they are learning and make the faith connections around relationships and sexuality.
  ○ As topics around sexuality are introduced, taught, and discussed, we continually connect that new knowledge with skills they can use in their everyday lives. The discussions and questions that we answer will make a concrete connection to our faith.
  ○ The program is a developmentally appropriate and creatively interactive approach to sexuality that places human sexuality in the context of faith. Adolescents respond to programs that give them new ways to look at their lives and the grace and space to explore their thoughts, feelings, and experiences. Middle-schoolers will receive reassurance that their growth and development is normal and expected. They need to know there is a place for them to ask their questions and receive honest answers.
  ○ Topics Include: Made in the Image of God, Self Image and Media, Love, Friendship and Infatuations, Biological Sex, Gender Identity, Gender Expression, Romantic Attraction, and Sexual Attraction, Sex as Fire, Biblical Models of Friendship, Refusal Skills, Prostitution and Pornography, Cyber Bullying, Sexually Transmitted Infections, Birth Control, Anatomy,

Assertive and Aggressive Behavior, Facts and Fiction around Sexuality, Decision-Making, Anatomy, Listening Skills, Value Clarification, and Faith Connection.

- The third goal is to empower you, the parents, to be the primary sexuality educators of their middle-schoolers:
  - The best way to help you make the connection between faith and sexuality is by inviting you and your middle-schoolers to learn and share at church. As a parent, it can be very difficult to address issues around puberty, development, and sexuality in a few conversations. The issues participants face and the questions they have are biological, social, spiritual, and cognitive and emotional. There will be a joint session with participants and parents (Session 8) that will give you the time and space to explore a range of issues together.

HOPE Ground Rules

Explain to parents:

- In keeping with the goal of empowering you, the parents, as the primary educators of your children, our Facilitator shares age-appropriate information with participants and encourages them to ask you—their parents—questions and to enter into conversations with you about the thoughts, feelings, and questions with which they wrestle.
- We recognize that there can be a wide range of beliefs and opinions about some controversial topics—including at church—so we seek to empower all of you to effectively teach your children about faith and sexuality.
- *These Are Our Bodies* aims to help you (a) clarify your values around faith and sexuality, (b) verbalize those values with and to your children, and (c) answer questions about difficult or sensitive topics.
- In the sessions, we establish a covenant for our time together to make sure we provide a safe place for participants to honestly and openly engage the content of the program. In the church, when we do our most important work, we often form what are called *covenant groups*. Covenant groups form to help members grapple with difficult topics and to grow together. The concept of covenant is a biblical one drawn from motifs in the Old Testament. In Genesis, we learn that God formed a covenant with Noah and set the rainbow in the sky as a reminder of that covenant. Also in Genesis, we hear the call for the people to be God's people in a deep covenant relationship. Today, we see covenants as promises between people.
- In *These Are Our Bodies*, we promise each other (covenant together) in our use of what we call the HOPE ground rules. HOPE is an acronym that stand for *Honesty, Openness, Privacy*, and *Enthusiasm*. Let us go over each aspect of the HOPE covenant:
  - **H** *stands for honesty:* In *These Are Our Bodies*, honesty is important. Participants will ask many questions; we (the Facilitator and Small-Group Leaders) promise to answer questions honestly. We will give participants the information they need in a way that they can understand. Participants promise to be honest about their questions and their feelings. The Facilitator and Small-Group Leaders make sure that the teaching and answers to questions are factual yet understandable to middle-schoolers.
  - **O** *stands for openness:* In *These Are Our Bodies*, being open is imperative for all to learn and grow. We want participants to be open to each other and their Small-Group Leaders. We want the group to use good listening skills to hear and respond to one another, both lovingly and respectfully. And we want to be open to the work of the Holy Spirit in and among us.

- *P stands for privacy:* Privacy is a core concept that helps participants feel comfortable as they share ideas and feelings. We want to hear about their experiences, and we ask that participants sharing experiences leave the names out of the story, which protects privacy. We also stress that what people share stays in this room. The Facilitator and Small-Group Leaders promise not to tell parents what individual participants say or do. *This piece is critical.* We may share with you what the group did or a summary of a discussion, but we will not share details about any one participant. Even so, one of our underlying commitments is to the safety of the children in our care. When working with children, leaders might wonder when the promise of confidentiality or privacy should be broken. The safety of the child or of other people trumps confidentiality. If we (the Facilitator or Small-Group Leaders) suspect that the child has been harmed, will be abused, will hurt themselves, or may cause harm to others, we will act immediately. In such cases, we will report our concerns to both clergy and Child Social Services. We let participants know about this exception to the privacy and confidentiality rule when we explain the HOPE ground rules in Session 1.

- *E stands for enthusiasm:* We ask that everyone involved in *These Are Our Bodies* to enter into it with a spirit of fun and wonder. The word enthusiasm comes from the root word *entheos* meaning "to be inspired by God."[11] The spirit of God is in and amongst us. The story of creation, the gift of sexuality, and the blessings of relationships are also filled with wonder—definitely a reason to be enthusiastic!

- Here is the HOPE litany as we share it in the GATHER portion of every session:

Honesty: We commit to sharing what we really think.
Openness: We commit to being open to what others say, both our group members and our leaders, and most of all to God.
Privacy: We commit to keeping what is said and done here within this space.
Enthusiasm: We commit to laughter, fun, and a sense of wonder.

Parents Are Key

Divide parents into groups of three or four. Say to groups:
- Turn to page 177 in the *Foundations Book*.
- We are going to have everyone read Chapter 21 titled Parents Are the Key. After you have read the chapter, discuss the questions on page 180 (in the *Foundation Book*) with your small group.
- We will spend 25 minutes on this portion of our session. I will keep time for us and let you know when we have about 5 minutes remaining. After your discussions, we will regather to share insights.
- As you discuss the questions, record your insights or takeaways in the space provided in your *Parent Book*. The Preview Session is found on pages 11–17.

When the time is up, call everyone together and continue:
- What takeaways did you have from your reading and discussion?

11 http://www.oxforddictionaries.com/us/definition/american_english/enthusiasm. (entheos 'possessed by a god, inspired,' based on *theos* 'god')

Record key points on easel paper for later reference. Writing down insights also honors parents' contributions and helps them to feel heard.

Say:
- Let's look at the schedule for *These Are Our Bodies*.

Distribute the schedule for the 10 sessions. If you haven't had parents register yet, pass out the registration form as well. Point out the dates and times of the session and emphasize that parents will need to participate in the parent portions of the program.

Ask:
- What questions do you have about the schedule or registration?

The Importance of Listening
Say to parents:
- One of the skills that we need as parents to navigate the changing needs of our families is listening.
- In our culture, it can sometimes feel like a lost art, yet it is imperative to a healthy family life.
- Let's spend some time refreshing ourselves on the importance of listening.
- Turn to page 14 in your *Parent Books*. Take a few seconds to read through these two quotes about listening. *(Pause as parents read, then continue:)*
- Which of these statements resonate with you?
- How can listening help your relationship with your child—and with your family?

After a few minutes of discussion, invite parents to silently review the PACK: Hints for Listening, found on pages 14–16 of their books. Invite them to spend some time reflecting on these hints and to use the space provided in their books to record their thoughts and feelings.

Discuss:
- How might applying these hints help you in your relationship with your middle-schooler?

Answering Questions

Say to parents:
- Now we are going to learn about answering questions.
- Turn to page 197 in the *Foundation Book* and read Chapter 25, titled *A Framework to Answer Questions*. After you have read the chapter, return to your small groups to discuss the questions found on page 205 (of the *Foundation Book*).
- We will spend 25 minutes on this portion of our session. I will keep time for us and let you know when we have about 5 minutes remaining. After your discussions, we will regather to share insights.

When the time is up, call everyone together and continue:
- What takeaways did you have from your reading and discussion?

After time for discussion, invite parents to practice using both their listening skills and their new way of answering questions. Say:

- Form new groups of three and roleplay answering a real middle-schooler's question.
- One person in each group will play the *teen*, one the *parent,* and the other the *observer*.
- Use the steps outlined in Chapter 25 of the *Foundation Book* to answer the question.
- Your question for the roleplay is: *What is rape and is it sexual abuse?*

Allow 5 minutes for the roleplay, then regather and ask these small groups to share how things went:

- How did it go?
- How well did you listen?
- How well were you able to incorporate the steps in answering questions?

Remind parents:

- You will have lots of opportunity to practice your skills in the next few weeks at home. Try out this new method. You will be surprised how well it works!

Invite any final questions before concluding the session.

Prayer

Say:

- Let us close with prayer.

    Leader: The Lord be with you.
    Parents: And also with you.
    Leader: Let us pray.

    Teach me to listen, O God, to those nearest me, my family, my friends, my co-workers.

    Help me to be aware that no matter what words I hear, the message is, "Accept the person I am. Listen to me."

    Teach me to listen, my caring God, to those far from me—the whisper of the hopeless, the plea of the forgotten, the cry of the anguished.

    Teach me to listen, O God my Mother, to myself. Help me to be less afraid to trust the voice inside in the deepest part of me.

    Teach me to listen, Holy Spirit, for your voice—in busyness and in boredom, in certainty and doubt, in noise and in silence.

    Teach me, Lord, to listen. *Amen*.[12]

---

12   Harter, Michael. *Hearts on Fire: Praying with Jesuits* (St. Louis: Institute of Jesuit Sources, 1993), 30.

Here, for leader's reference, are the *PACK: Hints for Listening* included in the *Parent Book:*

P*ay Attention*: turn to face your teen, open up your body and avoid crossing your arms. Simone Weil wrote, "Attention is the rarest and purest form of generosity."[13]

A*ffirm*: Give affirming nonverbals like head nodding and eye contact.

C*larify*: Repeat back what you are hearing using facts and the feelings your middle-schooler may be experiencing. At this age, especially, they need help identifying their feelings. When they are trying to communicate, they often use words like *angry, mad, sad,* or *happy* to describe their emotions. You can help by identifying their underlying feelings by giving them words like, *frustration, betrayal,* or *joy*. You could say, "It sounds like you feel_____, when _____ happens." Because this statement is a best guess at what they are thinking and feeling, allow your child to correct or revise your estimate. In this process, kids learn to value both their emotions and the details of an event.

K*eep*: Keep the conversation going by using open-ended statements like:
- I am interested in hearing what happened.
- I am here. I am listening. I have the time.
- Tell me more about that.

Use *statements*, which keep the emphasis on the person talking, instead of *questions*, which shift the focus back to you.

....

13   Foer, Jonathan Safran. *"How Not to Be Alone." The New York Times*, June 8, 2013.

SESSION 1

YOU ARE GOD'S CREATION

To say that I am made in the image of God is to say that love is the reason for my existence, for God is love. Love is my true identity. Selflessness is my true self. Love is my true character. Love is my name.[14]

— Thomas Merton

....

14 Merton, Thomas, *Seeds of Contemplation* (NY: New Directions Publishing Company, 1961), 46.

OBJECTIVES

- ❏ Participants will discover God's declaration of "very good" in the story of creation.
- ❏ Participants will analyze scripture passages related to the human body.
- ❏ Participants will begin to claim the adjectives "beautiful" and "wonderful" for themselves.
- ❏ Participants will know they are made in the image of God.[15]

SUPPLIES

- ❏ pencils or pens (1 per participant)
- ❏ *These Are Our Bodies Middle School Participant Books* (1 per participant)
- ❏ *These Are Our Bodies Middle School Leader Guides* (1 for the Facilitator and 1 for each Small-Group Leader)
- ❏ HOPE[16] poster (See pp. 13–14 and 35–36 for a description of the poster and its use. Download, print, and assemble the HOPE poster found online at the *These Are Our Bodies* Middle-School *Leader Guide* page: https://www.churchpublishing .org/theseareourbodiesmsleader. You will want to keep the poster up in the room to refer to during each session.)
- ❏ highlighters
- ❏ easel paper
- ❏ timer or stopwatch (a cell phone works well)
- ❏ Category Slips for the Game (Download from the These Are Our Bodies MIddle-School Leader Guide page: https://www.churchpublishing.org/ theseareourbodiesmsleader.), printed and cut apart

---

15 The first creation story uses the words *male* and *female* in relationship to creating humans. Although we use that biblical passage as the foundation for the theme of creation in God's image, we are aware and concerned by the limitation of the labels of male and female. In interpreting the scripture we see teaching of being "made in the image of God" to be affirming and uplifting, especially to young people who are searching for their identity. Although, for many of our friends, brothers, and sisters who do not identify with the binary language of male and female, the news of just two options misses the mark. Seeking to understand the Genesis text in light of the expansiveness of the gospel is helpful here. Being made in the image of God is being formed in the likeness of God. The description of male and female characterizes all of human kind, not only specific individual people.

The passage below from the Standing Commission on Liturgy and Music expands on those ideas: "Even the language of "same-sex" and "different-sex" raises many complex questions, not only biologically, socially, and culturally, but also and especially biblically.

Genesis 1 and 2, for example, are often cited to support two interrelated convictions: first, that "gender complementarity" describes God's creation of human beings as male and female; and second, that such complementarity is best expressed in the procreation of children within monogamous marriage. The extensive biblical scholarship available on these passages—in both Jewish and Christian tradition—nuances those two convictions in some important ways.

In the first of the two creation accounts (Genesis 1:26–27), gender differentiation is attributed to the whole human species rather than to individuals, just as both male and female alike apply to God, in whose image humanity is made. Similarly, the command to "be fruitful and multiply" (Genesis 1:28) is given to the human species, not to each individual. If this were not the case, people "who are single, celibate, or who for whatever reason do not have children—including Jesus of Nazareth"—would be viewed as "disobedient sinners." Moreover, the generative aspects of a loving and faithful commitment can be seen in many different ways, not only in bearing and raising children. For same-sex couples, as one Episcopal bishop has pointed out, "the care and nurture of those already in the world may be a mission more excellently fulfilled by those who do not have the concerns of child-rearing" (p. 34, Standing Commission on Liturgy and Music).

16 The authors have done their best, without success, to track down the original source of the HOPE acronym. No copyright infringement is intended. If notified, they will gladly credit the original author in future editions of *These Are Our Bodies*.

NOTES

_____

_____

_____

- ❏ small basket or bowl
- ❏ strips of paper
- ❏ scrap pieces of colored paper
- ❏ Question Box (See directions, pp. 14–17.)
- ❏ nametags
- ❏ *optional:* personal white boards and dry-erase markers, 1 per participant (These boards can be bought inexpensively in the fall during school-supply season for $1–$2 each.)

PREPARATION

- ❏ The Facilitator will divide the groups before the session starts and assign two leaders to each group. Each group should have 4–6 participants of different genders and from different schools. The Facilitator will want to think about the formation of the groups to ensure that cliques are not formed. Use the nametags to delineate the groups; for example, one group could have a blue border on the nametags and the other red. Another way is to put a different sticker on the nametags; for example, use star stickers for one group and happy-face stickers for another. Setting up the groups before the session saves time and helps the session go more smoothly. If you have 4–6 participants, do the activities as one group.
- ❏ Gather needed supplies.
- ❏ Set up the room for the session. Arrange furniture and materials so that they are readily available and designed for discussion. If you can clear part of the room to have participants sit on the floor during the discussion that will be helpful. Having participants and the Small-Group Leaders on the floor helps to create a warm environment and feels more relational than working at tables throughout the whole session.
- ❏ Read through the entire session. Jot down your own notes and prompts.
- ❏ Review the HOPE Ground Rules introduction.
- ❏ Review the explanation of the Question Box (pp. 14–17).
- ❏ Create the nametags for the participants and the Small-Group Leaders.

SUGGESTIONS

- ❏ Asking participants to be honest requires adults to be honest. If you do not know an answer, tell participants that you will find the answer. Then find and share the answer! Stress that you are committed to finding out answers to all of their questions. Make sure they know that you love questions.
- ❏ Privacy is especially important to young people. Assure them that (a) they can speak to you about anything without fear and (b) though you will share with parents how sessions unfold and what the group says, no individual names will be shared with parents.
- ❏ Making these sessions fun requires a fun approach and light-hearted demeanor. Be sure to make it a point to keep it this way during each session.

GATHER

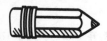

 20 minutes

Welcome all participants and leaders.

HOPE Poster

Direct attention to the HOPE poster. For this first session, you may want to hold a short discussion (see pp. 13–14 and 26) to expand what participants think each of the letters and statements on the poster mean. Refer to pages 13–14 and 35–26 in this *Leader Guide* for a full explanation of the HOPE poster.

Say:

- Every session we will begin with the same gathering ritual.
- The first purpose of this regular ritual is to remind us of the common ground that we want to maintain every time we meet.
- The second purpose is to remind us of the foundation for all that we will study: *our faith.*
- In the beginning, it may seem awkward and unnecessary, but after a few sessions you will find this is a good reminder of what we can expect from each other and what we should expect of ourselves.
- You can either read from the poster, or you can read from your *Participant Book*, where you will find the same content on page 8.
- I invite you to join me now by standing as we join in our opening ritual.

Lead the group in reading the words of the HOPE Poster together:

Honesty: We commit to sharing what we really think.
Openness: We commit to being open to what others say, both our group members and our leaders, and most of all to God.
Privacy: We commit to keeping what is said and done here within this space.
Enthusiasm: We commit to laughter, fun, and a sense of wonder.

Prayer

Lead participants in this prayer:

> Holy God, one who took on flesh and lived as one of us,
> dwell with us here and give us courage to learn, grow, and become more like you—
> loving, kind, and full of grace—
> through God our Creator, Christ our Redeemer,
> and the Spirit our Sustainer. *Amen*.

The Question Box

Note: Be sure you have read the full explanation of the Question Box found on pages 14–17 of the Introduction.

Show the Question Box, created before the session, as well as the pencils and scrap paper to be used to write questions. (Remember that each session should have its own color of paper.)

Explain:
- This is our Question Box. It is a place for you to submit any and all questions you already have or will soon have about sex, sexuality, gender, faith, etc.
- At different times you will have the opportunity to write questions for the box, so think about questions you might already have, even before we start. Maybe you have a joke or a word that you don't understand. Maybe a friend asked you a question and you want to submit it.
- We will always give you honest answers . . . or promise to find the answers.
- Everyone will write a question for the Question Box.
- We will use the Question Box at different times as we study and learn together.
- You will have an opportunity to write a question for the Question Box at the end of this session.

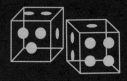

GAME

Good, Good, Very Good

 **20 minutes**

For each session's Game, consider moving the group to an alternative location—another area of the same room, another room, a space outdoors, etc. Young people benefit from movement and a change of seating.

In Session 1, the game is based on the scripture passage found in Genesis 1. The passage portrays God as the creator of all. At the end of each day of creation, God declares what has been created "good." Playing this game before reading the passage sets the stage for further discussion later in the GRAPPLE portion of the session. Therefore, *do not* make the connection for participants that the game is based on the passage. The most beautiful connections occur naturally and without prompting.

During the game, *each* participant will record *one* of their answers to reveal later to the group. Scraps of paper and pens are sufficient, but a small white board and dry erase marker for each participant will also work.

Directions for Good, Good, Very Good:
Begin by placing the Category Slips in the bowl or basket.

Explain:
- When it is your turn, draw a slip of paper from the bowl (basket). On that slip of paper you will find a category of "thing," for example, *cars, ice cream flavors, songs*. Your job is to think of three items that fit your category, two you think are "good" and one that you think is "very good."
- It is your individual decision which of the three items is "very good." You will need to write down all three of your items on a piece of paper, circling the one item that you think is "very good."

- Once everyone has thought of their three things and written them down (and circled their "very good" things), you will be asked, one at a time, to name your three things out loud to the group in any order. The group will then vote on which one they think you think is "very good."
- After everyone has voted, you will let the group know which of your things you selected as "very good." Because the group is learning about each other, you may also choose to explain why that item is "very good."
- Here is an example:
  - If I pulled the slip with the category *Desserts*, I might write down "ice cream, cake, and chocolate."
  - Because I am particularly fond of ice cream, that's the one I would circle as "very good."
  - When it's my turn, I would say to the group, "Cake, chocolate, and ice cream."
  - The leader would ask the group: Who votes for cake? Who votes for chocolate? Who votes for ice cream?
  - After everyone has voted, I would reveal my choice of ice cream and explain that though I like cake and chocolate, ice cream is *very good* because it comes in so many flavors and can be made into milkshakes, sundaes, smoothies, and more.

After everyone has had a turn, you can repeat with more rounds of the same or move on to the next section of the session (GRAPPLE). Be sure to have someone monitor the time or set an alarm to keep on task. Depending on the size of your group, you may have time for each person to do one category or you may be able to play multiple rounds.

At the end of the game, have participants and leaders remain at the location of the game to hear the directions for the next section.

GRAPPLE

NOTES

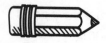

 45 minutes

Notes for Small-Group Leaders:
- Middle-schoolers who have spent time in church may have heard the scripture passages in this session before. What is unlikely is that they considered them directly related to human sexuality.
- Be sensitive to and aware of students who might not have experience with reading the Bible. Avoid questions that focus a literal interpretation of the text. Middle-schoolers will be able to see the broader themes and metaphors in the text. We use scholarship, our reasoning, and our faith when reading the Bible.
- Laying the theological foundation for human sexuality is essential to this program. Take the time now to make faith connections from the very beginning and your sessions will naturally continue down that path.
- When you get to the questions below, you will find each of them followed with commentary. This commentary provides the information you may need to help participants answer the questions. Share as little or as much of this as you feel is appropriate. *By all means, read through this section ahead of time to help you prepare!*

The Facilitator says:
- Now we are going to break into small groups.
- In your small groups you will need highlighters (1 per person), your *Participant Books* (1 per person), Bibles (1 per person), a piece of easel paper and at least one marker.

The Facilitator divides the groups as planned before the session (p. 43). When groups have gathered at their tables, Small-Group leaders designate a member of their group as the materials collector and sends that person to get supplies. At the end of GRAPPLE, the same person returns the supplies.

Once groups have settled in at their tables with their Small-Group Leaders and the needed supplies, the Facilitator walks from group to group throughout the remainder of GRAPPLE. The Facilitator's proximity to the small groups helps them stay on task. It also allows Small-Group Leaders to quickly solicit the Facilitator's help if they feel stuck or unsure. The Facilitator should be careful not to stay with any one group for too long. She or he is also responsible for keeping up with the time; setting a timer for 45 minutes ensures the session stays on track.

Small-Group Leaders say:
- Turn in your *Participant Books* to page 9 and in your Bible to Genesis 1. Genesis is the very first book of the Bible and is part of the Old Testament. When you have found both of those, hold up your pen or pencil so that I know you are ready.
- As we read these verses, listen for something important that is repeated.
- We can take turns reading the passage by reading some and then passing it on to the next person. If you do not want to read aloud, just say "Pass" or only read a short amount.

Read Genesis 1 aloud. The *Participant Books* only contain selected verses from Genesis 1. It is important, therefore, to begin by reading this entire chapter from the Bible.

Small-Group Leaders continue:
- You will find some verses from Genesis 1 in your *Participant Book* on pages 9–10. Using your highlighter, mark the phrase that you see repeated over and over. If you have not yet found it, hold up your pen and I will come and help you.

Here, for your reference, are the verses found in the *Participant Book:*
- Genesis 1:4a — "And God saw that the light was good" *(NRSV).*
- Genesis 1:10 — "God called the dry land Earth, and the waters that were gathered together he called Seas. And God saw that it was good" *(NRSV).*
- Genesis 1:12 — "The earth brought forth vegetation: plants yielding seed of every kind, and trees of every kind bearing fruit with the seed in it. And God saw that it was good" *(NRSV).*
- Genesis 1:17–18 — "God set them in the dome of the sky to give light upon the earth, to rule over the day and over the night, and to separate the light from the darkness. And God saw that it was good" *(NRSV).*
- Genesis 1:21 — "So God created the great sea monsters and every living creature that moves, of every kind, with which the waters swarm, and every winged bird of every kind. And God saw that it was good" *(NRSV).*
- Genesis 1:25 — "God made the wild animals of the earth of every kind, and the cattle of every kind, and everything that creeps upon the ground of every kind. And God saw that it was good" *(NRSV).*

Small-Group Leaders continue:
- Humanity is created *last.* The *Common English Bible* translation offers an especially beautiful account of these two important verses, Genesis 1:26–27. Look in your *Participant Books* to read these verses on page 10.

Then God said, "Let us make humanity in our image to resemble us so that they may take charge of the fish of the sea, the birds in the sky, the livestock, all the earth, and all the crawling things on earth." God created humanity in God's own image, in the divine image God created them, male and female God created them . . .

- Would someone volunteer to read the *New Revised Standard Version* translation of the same two verses, Genesis 1:26–27? Look in your *Participant Books* to read these verses, found on page 10.

  Then God said, "Let us make humankind in our image, according to our likeness; and let them have dominion over the fish of the sea, and over the birds of the air, and over the cattle, and over all the wild animals of the earth, and over every creeping thing that creeps upon the earth." So God created humankind in his image, in the image of God he created them; male and female he created them . . .

- Once God creates humankind, the phrase changes a bit. You may have already seen it, but put your finger on verse 31.

Ask a volunteer to read this aloud:

God saw everything that he had made, and indeed, it was very good (NRSV).

Continue:
- What do you notice that is different? *(Yes, it's the addition of the word* very *to God's declaration of* good. *Interestingly, the phrase* very good *does not specifically follow the creation of humanity; it is not until humankind is created, commanded to "be fruitful and multiply," and told to tend to the rest of creation that the double adjective is used.)*

Say:
- People have pondered this chapter of the Bible for a very long time. You may have been told this story as a young child from a picture book.
- What do you notice now that you did not notice then? Or, if you are hearing it for the first time, what stands out from this passage?

Give participants the opportunity to discuss the passage freely. Resist the urge to debate *how* creation occurred, instead redirecting group members to *who* created.

Say:
- Some words in this story are challenging or unfamiliar; other words are used in an unfamiliar way.
- Look again at the beginning of the passage Genesis 1:26–27 for the word *image* that is used in an unfamiliar way. For example, what is an "image"?

The Bible is full of metaphors and word play. *Image* here is not the same thing as what some participants may first think, especially as they are moving from concrete thinking to abstract thinking. Another word for *image* is *likeness*. You can also use the word *resemble* from the *CEB* translation.

Ask:

- Who is created in God's image? How does God create them? *(humankind, both male and female)*

Humankind is not just male or female, but both. Humankind embodies both male and female and is not complete without both male and female. They are also equal—one is not subordinate to the other.

Be careful not to place the emphasis on gender but instead on what is called *imago dei,* or the image of God. Try to use the word *humankind* instead of *mankind*.

Ask:

- What does it mean to "be fruitful"? What different meanings might this phrase have?[17]

The setting of the initial chapters of Genesis is vividly described. The words *be fruitful* play with the images of God's work of creation and with the garden in which the first human beings dwelled. The author of this passage seems especially concerned with the future of that which was created. *Fruitfulness* in this sense is that manifestation of love that bears witness to the love of God for all creation through Christ.

Fruitfulness today may not be the same as fruitfulness for the author of Genesis 1. According to Margaret Farley in her book *Just Love: A Framework for Christian Sexual Ethics,* "Traditional arguments that if there is sex it must be procreative have changed to arguments that if sex is procreative it must be within a context that assures responsible care of offspring."[18]

Farley goes on to note that offspring alone are not enough; instead, the reader must consider fruitfulness that is rooted in interpersonal love. She describes this kind of love as that which is open to the wider community of persons, that which "brings new life to those who love."[19]

We see this same command repeated after the flood in Genesis 8:17 and Genesis 9:1. In that passage it also seems important to the author that God's creation, God's *very good* creation, spread over the entire earth, an earth that has nothing else yet in it.

Ask:

- Are humans alone given the command to be fruitful?

Look back at verse 22 to identify the jobs that humans are given.

Ask:

- What were the first two humans supposed to do?

....

17 We also invite you to expand on the application of fruitfulness in this context to not only procreation but a fruitfulness of God's love. Our lives are fruitful as we manifest the love of God in our lives. Perhaps this could also echo the fruit of the spirit passage in Galatians 5:22–23 when a life lived in the spirit bears the spiritual fruit of love, joy, peace, patience, kindness, generosity, faithfulness, gentleness, and self-control.

18 Farley, Margaret. *Just Love: A Framework for Christian Sexual Ethics* (New York: The Continuum International Publishing Group Inc., 2006), 226–227.

19 Ibid, 227.

Make more humans and live in loving relationships with one another. Genesis 1:28a *(NRSV)* states, "God blessed them, and God said to them, 'Be fruitful and multiply, and fill the earth and subdue it.'"

Ask:
- Now that the earth is "filled" with people, does this command still apply in the same way?
- Why was it important to this story for the first humans to create more humans?

First, it is important to decide on the genre of Genesis 1. Even when the story is read as a historical account, there is room to see how not every human being must create more human beings in the modern day context. Many Christians choose to read this passage as myth. When taken as a myth, this story is no less meaningful to people who read it now than when it was first spoken as oral tradition.

One of the beauties of the Bible is its ability to continuously impact its reader, no matter the time in history it is read. As modern day readers, this passage should spur us on to modern day fruitfulness. Some might take that to mean taking care of God's creation. Others might emphasize taking care of the least in society. Later, in the New Testament book of Galatians, the term *fruit* is applied to what those who live by the Spirit do. It states, "By contrast, the fruit of the Spirit is love, joy, peace, patience, kindness, generosity, faithfulness, gentleness, and self-control. There is no law against such things . . ." (Galatians 5:22–23, *NRSV*).

Ask:
- What does the word *multiply* mean? How does it differ from the first command to *be fruitful*?

These two verbs are linked together in the command. Whereas fruitfulness may include many possible results such as was discussed in the quote from Margaret Farley, multiplying seems focused on increasing the sheer number of people on the earth. Therefore, in a most literal sense, multiply means to have babies.

Ask:
- Why do you suppose God declared everything "very good" after creating human beings? Is there something special about them compared to the rest of creation?

Human beings are created in the image of God. The rest of creation does not have this special mark. Human beings were created to be in relationship with God.

Ask:
- Does God know about our bodies?

If God created them, surely God knows all about them! The same way that you know all about something you create, God knows about the human body.

Ask:
- What does God think about our bodies?

In Genesis 1:28a it states, "God blessed them." Humanity was special enough to deserve a blessing! Beyond the blessing, God gave a special declaration. After creating humanity the Bible states, "God saw everything that he had made, and indeed, it was very good" (Genesis 1:31a *NRSV*). The change from *good* to *very good* is evidence of God's delight.

Ask:
- Do you think God knows about sex?

Yes, God knows about sex. God gave the command to create more human beings, which within the context and time of the story was only possible through sexual intercourse. Interestingly, though readers of the Genesis passage today know that babies are formed as a result of sexual intercourse, the author of the passage may not have understood that link so clearly (there is debate about how much ancient cultures understood about sex and pregnancy). Knowledge of human anatomy and human reproduction continues to advance even after many years of scientific study.

Be careful not to overemphasize that sex was designed within the binary of male and female. Later, when a future session discusses the differences between gender identity, gender expression, sexual attraction, and biological sex, it will be important that the creation of humanity as male and female does not limit attraction to between the opposite sex.

Ask:
- Does God know how babies are made? How do we know?

Yes, God knows how babies are made. It was God's idea!

GUIDE

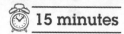
NOTES

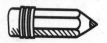

> ### The Facilitator leads this portion of the session.

Pass out small pieces of paper to each participant. Explain:
- Each of you will be writing a question for the Question Box, as you will be asked to do in every session. This is a great place to have your questions answered.
- Everyone needs to write a question. For example, you might ask about a word that you've heard but don't understand or a joke that you don't get. If you don't have a question of your own, think of a question that might be asked by someone your age.
- The Small-Group Leaders and the Facilitator will answer your questions at the beginning of the next session.

The Facilitator moves around the room with the Question Box to collect the questions.

After everyone has submitted a question, invite all participants (leaders and participants) to join in a large enough space where you can form a circle. After you have made the circle, invite everyone to move close enough to each other that they are touching shoulder to shoulder. Invite everyone to relax and take a deep breath. As they relax, they should naturally stop touching shoulders so closely yet maintain an appropriate level of intimacy for this portion of the session.

Invite all in the circle to close their eyes for a few seconds and slow their breathing. Maintain this for about 30 seconds.

Say:
- When we open our eyes and look again at the beauty of the group, pay special attention to those standing to your left and to your right. Let's take just a few more seconds, with our eyes closed, to enjoy the peacefulness of our community together. *(Pause.)*

- Open your eyes.
- Today we learned about the image of God imprinted on each one of us as a part of God's creation. We also learned that God views each one of us as very good and beautiful. Finally, we read God's command to be fruitful and multiply in Genesis chapter one.
- One way to be fruitful is to develop meaningful and loving relationships with others. Relationships like this require vulnerability. Vulnerability means letting others get close despite our fears or worries. It means opening ourselves up to each other, even the parts of ourselves that we struggle to call very good.
- A moment ago I asked you to pay special attention to the people to your immediate right and left. For this portion of our session we want to encourage one another.
- The person to your right will offer encouraging words to you and then you will offer encouraging words to the person on your left.
- I invite you to make a simple affirmation to the person beside you. "You are made in the image of God," is the short phrase we will use. Would someone like to volunteer to go first? Simply turn to the person on your left and say, "You are made in the image of God."

If no one volunteers, go first or prompt another adult/participant to go first whom you are confident will set the tone for the exercise. The goal is for everyone to feel encouraged.

When everyone has had a turn, the session is almost complete.

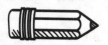 

NOTES

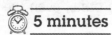

⏰ 5 minutes

The Facilitator leads this portion of the session.

Sending participants and leaders back into their daily lives is the final step in the session. This section is meant to be simple and quick.

Say:

- Leaving this time together requires a shift. This is a safe place. This is a place where we are learning and growing together. Outside of this place are our homes, schools, families, friends, and many other social circles.
- What I want to leave you with at the end of each session is that no matter where you are in the world, no matter who you are with, God is with you on your journey.
- Let us close with prayer:

  Leader: The Lord be with you.
  Participants: And also with you.
  Leader: Let us pray.

  O God, you made us in your own image and redeemed us through Jesus your Son: Look with compassion on the whole human family; take away the arrogance and hatred which infect our hearts; break down the walls that separate us; unite us in bonds of love; and work through our struggle and confusion to accomplish your purposes on earth; that, in your good time, all nations and races may serve you in harmony around your heavenly throne; through Jesus Christ our Lord. *Amen*.[20]

....

20 *Book of Common Prayer*, Prayer for the Human Family, page 815.

AFTER-THE-SESSION DEBRIEF

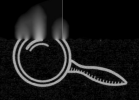

For Facilitator and Small-Group Leaders Only

 15–30 minutes

Goal:
- Debrief the session.
- Answer the questions from the Question Box from this session.
- Write the questions on easel paper to be used at the beginning of the next session.

Ask:
- What went well?
- How are participants doing?
- Are there any concerns that need to be addressed before the next session?

Say:
- Let's look at the questions from the Question Box.
- I will read each question one at a time. After I read the first question we will begin our process of considering the question.

Read the first question.

Ask:
- What is this person asking?
- What does a child this age need to know about this topic?
- How do we want to answer that question?
- Who would like to answer this question next week in front of the participants?

The group decides *how* to answer the questions before deciding *who* will answer. This gives the group more influence over the answer. The Facilitator makes notes on each question card of "talking points" that the group has mentioned.

When you are deciding who will answer the questions, have different people answer similar questions. If, for example, you have three questions on shaving, have three different Small-Group Leaders answer them. You could have a different aspect of the questions answered each time.

Once all of the cards are read and have been assigned to Small-Group Leaders, ask a Small-Group Leader to copy all of the questions onto the easel paper. Reword questions if they are confusing; correct spelling. Add the initials of each Small-Group Leader to the left of their assigned questions to remind you who will be answering which question during the next session.

The Facilitator should be prepared to volunteer for any questions that the Small-Group Leaders feel unprepared or uncomfortable answering.

Repeated questions should be expected. It takes 3–10 repetitions for participants to integrate these new vocabulary words and concepts into memory. For many participants, these concepts will be completely new. Be patient as the participants move from the first exposure to understanding the concepts.

Approach all questions with enthusiasm.

Assume good intent when answering the questions.

Try not to "condense" the questions or combine them. Participants will be looking for their specific question to be answered.

Refer to the Introduction (pp. 14–17, 30–31, and 63) for more explanation of the Question Box, including how to answer questions.

Small-Group Leaders and the Facilitator will want to read Chapters 1 and 2 in the *These Are Our Bodies Foundation Book* as a primary resource for answering participants' questions.

NOTES

SESSION 2

YOU ARE COMPLEX

You made all the delicate, inner parts of my body
and knit me together in my mother's womb.
Thank you for making me so wonderfully complex!
Your workmanship is marvelous—how well I know it.
—Psalm 139: 13–14, *NLT*

OBJECTIVES

❑ Participants will gain vocabulary about human sexuality that is non-binary and complex.[21]

❑ Participants will be able to define and differentiate between biological sex, gender identity, gender expression, and attraction.[22]

❑ Participants will begin to find clarity about their own biological sex, gender identity, gender expression, romantic attraction, and sexual attraction.

❑ Participants will recall they are created in the image of God.

❑ Participants will engage in discussion using new language about sexuality and gender.

SUPPLIES

❑ pencils or pens (1 per participant)

❑ *These Are Our Bodies Middle School Participant Books* (1 per participant)

❑ *These Are Our Bodies Middle School Leader Guides* (1 for the Facilitator and 1 for each Small-Group Leader)

❑ HOPE poster[23] (See pages 13–14; download at: https://www .churchpublishing.org/ theseareourbodiesmsleader.)

---

21 A note on the complexity of sexuality and the program: We offer this integrated and holistic way of understanding sexuality in response to the Episcopal church's growing understanding of the complexities of gender and gender orientation. We suggest using *LGBTQ+* (lesbian, gay, bisexual, transgender, and queer) when needed rather than other terms. We also recognize that the preferred language in the area of sexuality, orientation, and gender is fluid and dynamic. Our hope is to use language that expresses a deep respect and love for *all* people. If the language is interrupting that experience of *agape* love, change the language in the sessions to newer, more inclusive, language. For an exhaustive discussion, see the Standing Commission on Liturgy and Music Supplemental Materials for a discussion of sexual orientation and gender identity.

22 For more information on these terms, readers may find the following resources helpful: Some of this content is the combination of resources including information from a TEDx Talk by Dr. Margaret Nichols "Beyond the Binary: Understanding Transgender Youth" and the website http:// itspronouncedmetrosexual.com/2012/01/the-genderbread-person/., https://www.genderspectrum.org., http://www.glsen.org., http://geneq .berkeley.edu/lgbt_resources_definiton_of_terms.

23 The authors have done their best, without success, to track down the original source of the HOPE acronym. No copyright infringement is intended. If notified, they will gladly credit the original author in future editions of *These Are Our Bodies.*

NOTES

❏ easel paper and markers
❏ pictures for Show! Your! Board! Game (See directions on p. 64.)
❏ 2 sheets of poster board to make the Puzzle Activity (See directions on pp. 69–70.)
❏ Copy and cut apart the Puzzle Cards, 1 set per small group (See pp. 206–210 of the Appendix.)
❏ copy of Answer Key (pp. 211–212)
❏ scrap pieces of colored paper for the Question Box (3" x 5")
❏ Question Box (See directions, pp. 14–17.)
❏ nametags: Divide participants into groups of 6–8 with a diversity[24] of leadership and participants in each group. Use a different border on the nametags or a sticker to differentiate the groups.
❏ *optional:* personal white boards and dry-erase markers, 1 per participant (These boards can be bought inexpensively in the fall during school-supply season for a $1–$2 each.)
❏ 8½" x 11" blank paper for Show! Your! Board! (if you don't have white boards for each participant)

PREPARATION

❏ Gather needed supplies.
❏ Set up the room for the session. Arrange furniture and materials so that they are readily available and designed for discussion.
❏ Read through the entire session carefully to get acquainted with the language. This language is embedded throughout the remainder of the program. It may differ from language you have used before.

---

24 Diversity is the authors' attempt to use more inclusive language. Diversity includes age, gender identity, participants' schools, maturity levels, and extracurricular activities and interests.

GATHER

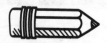

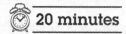 **20 minutes**

As participants enter, have them put on their nametags, pick up their *Participant Books,* and select a pencil or pen.

HOPE Poster

Gain participants' attention and say:
- Welcome everyone. As we begin today, *(name of participant)* is going to lead us in today's GATHER.
- Who would like to lead us next week?

Make a note of the volunteer for next week.

Participant says:
- Let's look together at our HOPE poster.
- Stand and join me as we read together:

Honesty: We commit to sharing what we really think.
Openness: We commit to being open to what others say, both our group members and our leaders, and most of all to God.
Privacy: We commit to keeping what is said and done here within this space.
Enthusiasm: We commit to laughter, fun, and a sense of wonder.

Prayer

Lead participants in this prayer:

> Holy God, one who took on flesh and lived as one of us,
> dwell with us here and give us courage to learn, grow,
>   and become more like you—
> loving, kind, and full of grace—
> through God our Creator, Christ our Redeemer,
> and the Spirit our Sustainer. *Amen.*

The Question Box

Note: Be sure you have read the full explanation of the Question Box found on pages 14–17 of the Introduction.

Say:
- Last week you had an opportunity to write a question for the question box. Thank you to everyone who was here last week and wrote a question.
- Your Small-Group Leaders and I are going to answer your questions. We have written the questions on easel paper so everyone can see the questions.

Hang the questions on the wall or tape the easel paper on the easel, then show the Question Box.

Say:
- Remember this is our Question Box. It is a place for you to submit any and all questions you already have or will soon have about sex, sexuality, gender, faith, etc.
- We will use the Question Box at different times as we study and learn together.
- Remember that each of you will be writing a *new* question for the Question Box in a few minutes.

The Facilitator reads one question and says:
- *(Small-Group Leader's name)* is going to answer that question.

Guidelines for answering questions:

- Think about the time that it will take to answer the questions. An average of 60–90 seconds per question is a reasonable guideline. Answering questions for a group of 6–8 participants will take 8–12 minutes.
- Adjust the amount of time that you allow based on your group.
- Do not over-explain. Keep it moving!
- Go down the question list one by one and answer each question. The Small-Group Leaders and the Facilitator will have already decided how to answer each question and who will answer the question at the end of last session.
- Remember to answer the questions clearly and concisely. You are aiming for a 45–60 second answer.
- Don't belabor the answers. You will want to spend as much time on the session as you can.

When all the questions have been answered, move into the GAME portion of the session.

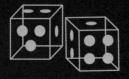

GAME

"Show! Your! Board!"

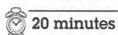 20 minutes

For each session's GAME, consider moving the group to an alternative location—another area of the same room, another room, a space outdoors, etc. Young people benefit from movement and a change of seating.

Show! Your! Board! requires visuals. Find pictures that play into gender stereotypes. Picture possibilities include a *ballet slipper*, a *basketball*, a *black dress suit*, a *chainsaw*, a *racecar*, a *red rose*, something *pink*, something *blue*, tube of *lipstick*, *athletic shoes, high heels*, etc.—objects that traditionally have been thought of as related to either males or females. As the session unfolds, participants will come to understand how, despite cultural stereotypes, gender is not as simple as two categories.

Try to choose actual photos (as opposed to clip art). You might be able to collect photos from advertisements in magazines. Each picture should be at least 8½" x 11", so the whole group can see the pictures when they are held up in the front of the room. Collect a total of 10 pictures.

This game helps participants think about how they have already been shaped by the culture around them. For example, if you show a picture of a ballet slipper and the majority of the participants write "female," you might ask, "What is it about a ballet slipper that makes you think of femininity? Can ballet be masculine, too?" If you show a picture of a racecar and the majority of participants write "male," you might ask, "What is it about a racecar that makes you think of men? Can women drive a racecar, too?"

The Facilitator leads this discussion with the group. Pause between questions and encourage conversation.

Directions for Show! Your! Board!

Participants sit in a circle so they can see the leader and each other. Make sure each participant has a small whiteboard and eraser *or* several sheets of blank paper and a marker, pen, or pencil.

Say:
- This is a game of word association.
- The results will help guide the discussion for the GRAPPLE portion of this session.
- When I show you a picture, you will respond by writing either the word "male" or "female."
- You will only have 5 seconds to record your answer. Keep your board hidden from those around you.
- We will reveal our answers all at once. As a group, we will shout, game-show style, "Show! Your! Board!" All at once, flip your boards to the front so everyone can see your answer.
- After each picture we will have a very short discussion.
- I will invite two people to speak about why they wrote their particular answers. I want you to pay attention to each other's answers. In the next part of our session we will talk more about our session title: *You Are COMPLEX*.
- Are you ready?

Wait until everyone has given a head nod of agreement or said "yes" before moving on.

Show the first picture. Say:
- 5, 4, 3, 2, 1
- "Show! Your! Board!" *(Prompt* everyone to say this out loud with you, one word at a time.)

Select a participant and ask:
- Why did you choose "male" (or "female") for this picture? Just give me a very short answer.

Select another participant and ask:
- Why did you choose "female" (or "male") for this picture? Just give me a very short answer.

Say:
- Erase your boards
- Ready?

Show the next picture. Repeat for all 10 pictures.

After all 10 pictures have been played, conclude the game with a conversation, using the questions below. There are no right or wrong answers. One of the objectives is to have the participants think about their gender as being non-dualistic—it is COMPLEX!

Ask:
- Do objects like ballet slippers, racecars, and high heels have a gender?
- Why do you think we connected a certain gender with these objects in the game?

- What role does our culture play in this connection?
- How do you feel about the cultural stereotypes of gender?
- Do you think it is possible for an object to be neutral or to have no gender connection?

Distribute pencils or pens. Make sure the participants have their Participants Books. *Say:*

- We are about to begin a discussion on how COMPLEX each of us is when it comes to our sexuality.
- Open up your *Participant Books* to page 15.
- I want you to think about the game we just played by answering the questions in your *Participant Book*. We are going to reflect on what you just experienced during this game for a few minutes as you complete the questions on page 16. After you finish reflecting, we will move to GRAPPLE.
- When you are ready to move on, signal that to me by putting down your pencil.

GRAPPLE

 45 minutes

Remember to read over this portion of the session carefully. Much of the information in this session will be new, not only to participants, but also to Small-Group Leaders (and quite possibly to you, the Facilitator). If necessary, take time in advance of the session to talk with Small-Group Leaders about this material to gain clarity and head off potential obstacles due to the newness of information covered.

Language is important when speaking with participants about gender. Consider how culture has already shaped the way *you* speak. Monitor your language and remember that speaking of gender as binary (either male or female, without any room for variation and ambiguity) excludes many individuals, all of whom are created in the image of God. One way to avoid gender pronouns such as *he* and *she* is to use the plural versions *they*, *their*, and *them*. The grammar may be incorrect, but the intention is spot on.

In this session we will introduce a COMPLEX way of talking about sexuality. We will practice using new ideas about sexuality that go beyond the constricting binary ideas of male and female or heterosexual or homosexual.

Gender identity, gender expression, attraction, and biological sex are thought by some to be *independent* of one another. We are coming to see all four aspects of sexuality as working together to form a COMPLEX view of sexuality. All four aspects of human sexuality form in different ways and can be at different ends of a continuum. The idea of a continuum is one way to discuss the complexity of human sexuality.

One analogy for the complexity of human sexuality is a mathematical metaphor. Consider each aspect of human sexuality as a line segment. Line segments have two distinct end points.

For biological sex, the two end points are what have traditionally been known as "male" and "female." Between the two endpoints are endless other points on the continuum. Each of these points is a place *between* male and female.

Participants are on different paths toward understanding their own sexuality. Some may have begun to understand or explore their sexuality; for others, exploration and questioning is still years away. Be sensitive to the clues that they give and lean toward openness and inclusion.

The idea of "coming out" is a cultural norm today. There is some writing about how people are coming out in a new way. The research suggests that modern young people see the labels of *gay, homosexual, bi-sexual,* and *transgender* as conforming to a narrow system.

This GRAPPLE has options for you to consider prior to teaching this session. Depending on your group's size, developmental readiness, maturity, and prior knowledge, it may be necessary to start with basic information and build. Other groups may exhibit signs of readiness for a more advanced set of information. As Facilitator, it is your job to make the best choice for your group. *Read ahead to prepare.*

Jay Emerson Johnson says this in the book *Peculiar Faith*:

> Today, the language of gay and lesbian desire visibly punctuates American culture . . . Many people in their late teens and early twenties now prefer to handle their sexual and gender identities a bit more lightly, resisting the cultural mechanism of indent labels. They seem to know, and perhaps only intuitively . . . Coming out as gay or lesbian depends on a preformative script, and younger generations today to resist scripted lives.[25]

The possibilities for biological sex, gender identity, gender expression, and attraction are infinite.[26] The complexity of sexuality compels us to challenge our language and our understanding around sexuality.

Here is an example of sexuality that is understood best on a continuum:

Biological Sex: A person is born with a vagina, ovaries, and two X chromosomes, therefore is declared biologically female.

Gender Identity: The person identifies as a woman.

Gender Expression: The individual expresses herself through stereotypically masculine ways.

Attraction: The same person is romantically attracted to both men and women, but sexually attracted to only women.

All four of these statements could apply to one individual.

---

25 Johnson, Jay Emerson, *Peculiar Faith: Queer Theology for Christian Witness* (NY: Seabury, 2014), 78.

26 *These Are Our Bodies* seeks to introduce and use inclusive language that seeks to meet the needs of all people. Language is always evolving. Here are a few terms that may be new to the leaders, but the participants or parents might know and use. *Agender* refers to a person who is internally ungendered or does not feel a sense of gender identity. *Cisgender* refers a person who by nature or by choice conforms to gender-based expectations of society. *Gender fluid* describes one who moves in and out of different ways of expressing and identifying oneself. *Intersex* refers to one who is born with chromosomes, external genitalia, or internal reproductive systems that do not fall into socially-constructed male and female ways of thinking about sex. And finally, *pangender* refers to someone whose gender identity if made up of all or many gender expressions.

Here is a second example:

Biological Sex: A person is born with a penis, testicles, and XY chromosomes, therefore declared biologically male.

Gender Identity: The person identifies as a woman.

Gender Expression: The person expresses to others in primarily feminine ways.

Attraction: The individual is attracted to women.

Though these two examples are somewhat helpful, they are also very limited.

Consider the ambiguity that often leads to what is called "sex assignment." According to Sally Lehrman, in her article "Going Beyond X and Y," "Genital ambiguity occurs in an estimated one in 4,500 births, and problems such as undescended testes happen in one in 100. Altogether, hospitals across the U.S. perform about five sex-assignment surgeries every day."[27]

Instead of direct instruction or lecture, this session will utilize a game—The Puzzle Game. This instructional strategy is important because the information is likely new to the participants. Therefore, move tables and chairs if necessary or go to a large open space. Sit on the floor if needed. (Remember that open snack concept!)

Two versions of the same game are given. Choose the level that is appropriate for your group:
- If you choose the simple level, there are five cards per term.
- If you choose the advanced level, there are thirteen cards per term (5 simple and 8 advanced). The advanced level must include both sets of cards the first time the game is played.

You can always revisit the advanced level at another time. In this case, you could play with 5 cards per category during this session and 8 cards per category on another day.

It is the discretion of the Facilitator and Small-Group Leaders to assess their participants for the GRAPPLE portion of this session.

Preparation for The Puzzle Game:
- You will need 2 sheets of poster board and thick felt markers.
- On one sheet of poster board enlarge the puzzle pieces as shown on the Puzzle Sheet found on pages 202–205 in the Appendix; write, on each of the four pieces, one of these four terms— *Biological Sex, Gender Identity, Gender Expression, Attraction*. Repeat for a second Puzzle Sheet.
- Photocopy on *card stock* (available at an office supply store) two sets of the Game Cards found on pages 206–210 of the Appendix. Cut these apart. Keep each set separate.
- The game is played with two groups; each will get an enlarged Puzzle Sheet and a set of Game Cards.

27 Lehrman, Sharon, "Going Beyond X and Y," Scientific American http://www.scientificamerican.com/article/going-beyond-x-and-y/.

- If you do not have enough participants for at least two teams, have everyone in one group with one Puzzle Sheet and one stack of Game Cards. The participants take turns picking up a card and placing it on the Puzzle Sheet. Play the game until all the cards have been played, then continue to the conversation after the game.
- Note that the Facilitator and Small-Group Leaders will all need a copy of the Answer Key found on pages 211–212 of the Appendix.

Instructions for The Puzzle Game:

Divide participants into two teams. Establish a home base for each team that is about 6' from its Puzzle Sheet.

Explain:

- This next portion of our session is a "race" between teams.
- Your stack of Game Cards contains statements that match the terms on the Puzzle Sheet.
- It is your job to read a card and place it on the appropriate puzzle piece on your Puzzle Sheet.
- The first team to accurately place all cards on its Puzzle Sheet wins.
- Each team begins at home base. *You may only read one card at a time.* A team member picks the top card and reads it out loud to the group. As a group, decide which piece of the puzzle it matches.
- The terms are: *biological sex, gender identity, gender expression*, and *attraction*.
- You can look at this poster, to remind yourself of the definitions.
- The person at the front picks up a card and reads it out loud. The team then confers to choose a puzzle piece.
- After you have decided as a group, the card reader takes the card to the Puzzle Sheet and sets it on top of the chosen section, being careful not to cover up the vocabulary term for the next person to see.
- The same pattern repeats until all the cards have been read, identified, and placed on a portion of the Puzzle Sheet.
- Remember, this is a race, but accuracy also counts. A Small-Group Leader will be waiting at your Puzzle Sheet to check for accuracy as you place your cards. To win, they also have to be on the correct term.
- If you have incorrectly placed a statement, the Small-Group Leader will send you back to your group to try again. At that point, the group chooses another puzzle piece.
- Before we begin, what questions do you have?

Make sure each team has a Small-Group Leader monitoring its Puzzle Sheet. The Small-Group Leader needs a copy of the Answer Key (Appendix, pp. 211–212). The Small-Group Leaders also watch to make certain:

- participants only read *one card at a time*
- small groups discuss each card *as a group*
- each card gets paced on the Puzzle Sheet *before moving on to the next card*

Complete the directions:

- Now, if your group does not finish first, that is okay. Once we have a winner, we will let the remaining groups finish so that they can still read and see the statements they have left.
- Is everybody ready? On your mark, get set, GO!

Allow the game to play through, watching for common errors in placement that can be discussed later during the second half of GRAPPLE. Resist discussing with participants what they are reading; allow them to discuss and ponder the cards on their own. Participants may have never heard of these vocabulary terms and the game is meant as a "fun" introduction.

If during the game you find that your group is especially new and becoming very frustrated, you may want to pause and move to the discussion portion sooner. This is okay. Participants come to these sessions with varying levels of prior knowledge. Highly competitive participants may need a reminder that this is just a game.

Discussing Biological Sex

Say:

- Now that you have placed the cards on the Puzzle Sheet, let's double-check and see what we observe and learn.

Ask participants to return to their seats. The next step will be to review the answers and confirm the correct placement of cards. Participants will now record the correct answers in their *Participant Books* and discuss the reasons why each statement belongs in a particular category.

Continue:

- Turn to page 18 in your *Participant Book*. There you will find a copy of the Puzzle Sheet.
- As I read over the explanations of each portion of the Puzzle Sheet, think back to where you put each card during the game. As we go, record the phrases or words on the next few pages. You can also take notes or write down questions for later.
- *Biological sex* refers to the physical anatomy of an individual's body. When a baby is born, doctors "assign" a sex to the baby based on the visible genitalia. For some babies, this is the presence of a vagina or a penis. For other babies, it is not as clear. That is why it is called an "assigned sex." A baby does not get a choice in what the doctor or parent assigns.
- You may not be aware that in some cases, when it is not clear to the doctor or parents, surgery is performed to make a decision on the baby's biological sex. More recently, some doctors have started asking whether this kind of decision should be made later on when a child is able to have a say.
- Let's see what statements went with the category "biological sex" on the Puzzle Sheet.

Discuss the stack of cards associated with "biological sex."

Say:

- *Male* and *female* are two words you probably already know. They are the terms doctors use to assign a biological sex to an infant at birth. When the testicles of a baby are not in the right place or if it is not clear whether the infant has a clitoris or a penis, someone is assigned a biological sex. Someone's assigned sex is what the doctor and parents write on the birth certificate based on what they determine from a physical examination. It is not based on internal organs or an analysis of the baby's genetics and hormones.

- *Genetic makeup* refers to whether scientific tests determine a person has *XX, XY,* or another makeup of chromosomes. Some *hormones* are produced in the ovaries or testes. *Physical anatomy* includes terms like penis, ovaries, vagina, and testicles.
- All of these statement or words fall into the category of "biological sex."
- What do these terms and phrases have in common?

Discussing Gender Identity

One Small-Group Leader now reads the stack of cards associated with *gender identity*.

Say:

- The second category is "gender identity." Unlike the "assigned sex," where an infant has no choice, gender identity is built upon what an individual *senses internally*. The two words *man* and *woman* are not used when talking about an infant for a reason. Infants grow into children who grow into adults. It is the phase of life you are in right now that begins to separate a child from an adult. Adolescence is the period in life where individuals *affirm their gender* based on what is *in their head.*
- An individual who does not have an internal sense that they are a man or a woman might say that they are *gender fluid*. Someone who does not feel like they fit in a specific category for gender might say they are *gender queer*. Gender identity is not necessarily the same as an individual's genitals or hormones. In other words, a person can have a penis and testicles but not the internal sense that they are a man. That individual's gender identity might be described as female. A person whose biological sex is not the same as their internal sense of gender might claim the term *transgender.*

Discussing Gender Expression

A Small-Group Leader reads the stack of cards associated with *gender expression*.

Say:

- Earlier we played a word association game related to gender. The results of that game should make this section of our session easier to understand. Remember how many of us associated high heels with being *feminine* and the color blue with being *masculine?* A person who wears high heels might do so to express their gender as more feminine. A person who likes to wear mainly blue might do so to express their gender as more masculine. Gender expression is *the way a person interprets their gender with outward displays of that gender stereotype*.
- You could also say that gender expression is a *visible display to the outside world*.

- Someone who is *gender nonconforming* chooses to express their gender in ways that are not stereotypical. For example, a male who wears lipstick or a female who likes to cut her hair very short.

Discussing Attraction

A Small-Group Leader reads the cards for *attraction*.

Say:

- The last category is *attraction*.
- Attraction refers to *when someone is physically drawn to another person or sees someone as desirable.*

The Facilitator continues and begins a conversation and discussion with the group.

Ask:

- What words or phrases stood out to you in this category?
- Do you think attraction is based on gender?
- Do you think attraction is based on biological sex?

Remember to empower the participants to voice their own thoughts and feelings. Young people need the grace and space to explore new ideas and values for themselves without judgment or the need to conform to those around them, including leaders.

Say:

- The title of this session is *You Are COMPLEX.*
- Most importantly, as we prepare to move into the GUIDE portion of our session, I want to remind you that you are created in the image of God. Humanity, in all of its complexities, is declared *very good* by the Creator.
- If you have questions about what we just covered, please write them down and put them in the Question Box.

GUIDE

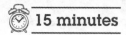 15 minutes

The Facilitator leads this portion of the session.

Pass out small pieces of paper to each participant. Explain:
- Each of you will be writing a question for the Question Box, as you will be asked to do in every session. This is a great place to have your questions answered.
- Everyone needs to write a question. For example, you might ask about a word that you've heard but don't understand or a joke that you don't get. If you don't have a question of your own, think of a question that might be asked by someone your age.
- The Small-Group Leaders and the Facilitator will answer your questions at the beginning of the next session.

The Facilitator moves around the room with the Question Box to collect the questions.

After everyone has submitted a question, invite all participants (leaders and participants) to join in a large enough space where you can form a circle. After you have made the circle, invite everyone to move close enough to each other that they are touching shoulder to shoulder. Invite everyone to relax and take a deep breath. As they relax, they should naturally stop touching shoulders so closely, yet maintain an appropriate level of intimacy for this portion of the session.

Invite all in the circle to close their eyes for a few seconds and slow their breathing. Maintain this for about 30 seconds.

Discuss:
- When we talk about God at church, we sometimes use the word *Trinity*. Does anyone know what that word means when we use it to talk about God?
- The word *Trinity* refers to the three persons of God: *Father, Son*, and *Holy Spirit*. Another expression of the same three persons is: *Creator, Redeemer*, and *Sustainer*.

- I wonder if at the end of this lesson it might be helpful for us to see God's image in ourselves in yet another way. Words in the English language fall very short in describing God. The Trinity is often called a holy mystery because it does not make sense to the human mind. How is it possible for 1 + 1 + 1 to equal 1?
- The same mystery is found in humanity. How is it possible to describe such a COMPLEX creation as humanity? Are words like *man* and *woman* enough?
- Think of it like this: If I only spoke of God as "Son," what would I miss out on? If I only saw God as "Father," how would I limit my understanding of God? If I only focused on the movement of God as the Holy Spirit, what would I not experience?
- Now think about yourself. If you speak of yourself as "male" or "female," do you feel like it is a limited viewpoint? If someone only allows you to express yourself in masculine ways or feminine ways, do you get to express your whole self?
- Just as God is COMPLEX, so is humanity. After all, we were created in the image of God.
- To help us close today, I want us to take turns looking at the person directly to our right and saying, "You are complex because you are made in God's image."
- Let's practice by saying it together once: *You are complex because you are made in God's image.*
- After everyone has had a turn to affirm their neighbor, encourage participants to write a question for the Question Box. Then move into the final portion of the session.

GO

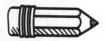

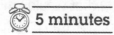 **5 minutes**

The Facilitator leads this portion of the session.

Sending participants and leaders back into their daily lives is the final step in the session. This section is meant to be simple and quick.

Say:
- Today's session included some really deep and COMPLEX ideas.
- If you have more questions or need clarification, please ask any adult or talk to your parents about it at home. Now, as always, I am aware that leaving this time together requires a shift. This is a safe place.
- This is a place where we are learning and growing together. Outside of this place are our homes, schools, families, friends, and many other social circles.
- Remember, no matter where you are in the world, no matter who you are with, God is with you on your journey.
- Let us close with prayer:

  Leader: The Lord be with you.
  Participants: And also with you.
  Leader: Let us pray.

  O God of peace, who has taught us that in returning and rest we will be saved, in quietness and confidence will be our strength: By the might of your Spirit lift us, we pray you, to your presence, where we may be still and know that you are God; through Jesus Christ our Lord. *Amen.*[28]

You might want to keep the poster of the terms from GRAPPLE in the room for the rest of the program. It will be helpful to revisit and refer to this material in the sessions that follow.

28 Adapted from the Book of Common Prayer, page 832.

AFTER·THE·SESSION
DEBRIEF

For Facilitator and Small-Group Leaders Only

Please see the full material found in Session 1, page 57.

 15–30 minutes

The time for this debrief will shift depending on the number and complexity of questions. Adjust the time for the debrief, if needed.

NOTES

SESSION 3

YOU ARE ACCEPTED

> To say that I am made in the image of God is to say that love is the reason for my existence, for God is love. Love is my true identity. Selflessness is my true self. Love is my true character. Love is my name.[29]
>
> — Thomas Merton

29 Merton, Thomas, *Seeds of Contemplation* (NY: New Directions Publishing Company, 1961), 46.

OBJECTIVES

❑ Participants will continue to claim the *Imago Dei*.
❑ Participants will discover God accepts them.
❑ Participants will examine cultural stereotypes of the human body.
❑ Participants will explore the connection between being accepted by God and the incarnation of God as Jesus.
❑ Participants will analyze their self-image.

SUPPLIES

❑ pencils or pens (1 per participant)
❑ *These Are Our Bodies Participant Books* (1 per participant)
❑ *These Are Our Bodies Leader Guides* (1 for the Facilitator and 1 for each Small-Group Leader)

❑ HOPE poster[30] (See pp. 13–14.)
❑ easel paper and markers
❑ scrap pieces of colored paper for the Question Box (3" x 5")
❑ Question Box (See directions, pp. 14–17.)
❑ nametags
❑ *optional:* personal white boards and dry-erase markers, 1 per participant (These boards can be bought inexpensively in the fall during school-supply season for a $1–$2 each.)
❑ timer
❑ assorted small objects, 1 per participant (The objects need to be three-dimensional, common, small objects, for example a pencil, a rubber ball, a coffee cup, a cell phone, a watch, etc. The size of an object should be small enough that one

30 The authors have done their best, without success, to track down the original source of the HOPE acronym. No copyright infringement is intended. If notified, they will gladly credit the original author in future editions of *These Are Our Bodies*.

NOTES

participant can hold it without the other participant seeing it.)

- ❑ bowl or bag to hold objects
- ❑ clipboards (1 per 2 participants)
- ❑ assorted magazines with photos of people, 2 per participant (*Details, Glamour, Vogue, People, GQ, Cosmopolitan, etc.*)
- ❑ glue sticks (1 per participant)
- ❑ scissors (1 per participant)
- ❑ sheets of plain white paper 8½" x 11" (1 per participant)
- ❑ computer or tablet with Internet access to play short video clip (with sound) (If you do not have Internet access, you may need to download the clip in advance. The link for the clip is within the session.)
- ❑ projector
- ❑ easel paper on which you have written the Question Box questions from Session 2
- ❑ painter's tape to hang the easel paper on the wall, if needed

PREPARATION

- ❑ Gather needed supplies.
- ❑ Set up the room for the session. Arrange furniture and materials so that they are readily available and designed for discussion.
- ❑ Put the small objects in the bag. Participants should not see the objects before the GAME.
- ❑ Prepare the easel paper for the collage before the session. Write on the top of the paper: *Made in the Image of God?* Keep this paper concealed until you start the GRAPPLE.
- ❑ Prepare to watch a short clip on the Internet. Test your connection and speakers before your session. You may want to ask a Small-Group Leader to be your technology expert for the session.

GATHER

NOTES

 20 minutes

As participants enter, have them put on their nametags, pick up their *Participant Books*, and select a pencil or pen.

HOPE Poster

Gain participants' attention and say:
- Welcome everyone. As we begin today, *(name of participant)* is going to lead us in today's GATHER.
- Who would like to lead us next week?

Make a note of the volunteer for next week.

Participant says:
- Let's look together at our HOPE poster.
- Stand and join me as we read together:

Honesty: We commit to sharing what we really think.
Openness: We commit to being open to what others say, including our group members, our leaders, and most of all to God.
Privacy: We commit to keeping what is said and done here within this space.
Enthusiasm: We commit to laughter, fun, and a sense of wonder.

Prayer

Lead participants in this prayer:

For Joy in God's Creation O heavenly Father, who has filled the world with beauty: Open our eyes to behold thy gracious hand in all your works; that, rejoicing in your whole creation, we may learn to serve you with gladness; for the sake of him through whom all things were made, your Son Jesus Christ our Lord. *Amen.*[31]

....

31 Adapted from Book of Common Prayer, page 814.

Say:

- Thank you *(name of participant)* for leading us in our GATHER.

The Question Box

Note: Be sure you have read the full explanation of the Question Box found on pages 14–17 of the Introduction.

Show the Question Box, created before the session, as well as the pencils and scrap paper to be used to write questions. (Remember that each session requires its own color of paper.)

Explain:

- This is our Question Box. It is a place for you to submit any and all questions you already have or will soon have about sex, sexuality, gender, faith, etc.
- As you know by now, we use the Question Box in each session.
- Today each of you will be writing a new question for the Question Box.
- Thank you to everyone who was here last week and wrote a question.
- Your Small-Group Leaders and I are going to answer your questions. We have written the questions on easel paper so everyone can see the questions.

Tape the questions to a wall and say:

- The Small-Group Leaders and I are going to answer your questions.

The Facilitator reads one question and says:

- *(Small-Group Leader's name)* is going to answer that question.

Repeat until all the questions have been answered.

Guidelines for answering questions:

- Think about the time that it will take to answer the questions. An average of 60–90 seconds per question is a reasonable guideline. Answering questions for a group of 6–8 participants will take 8–12 minutes.
- Adjust the amount of time that you allow based on your group.
- Do not over-explain. Keep it moving!
- Go down the question list one by one and answer each question. The Small-Group Leaders and the Facilitator will have already decided how to answer each question and who will answer the question at the end of last session.
- Remember to answer the questions clearly and concisely. You are aiming for a 45–60 second answer.
- Don't belabor the answers. You will want to spend as much time on the session as you can.

When all the questions have been answered, say:

- You all asked great questions.
- Remember that you will have an opportunity to write a question for the Question Box at the end of this session.

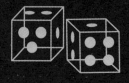

GAME

NOTES

Back to Back

 20 minutes

For each session's GAME, consider moving the group to an alternative location—another area of the same room, another room, a space outdoors, etc. Young people benefit from movement and a change of seating.

Invite participants to pair off, preferably with someone they do not know well. Ask them to find a place to sit on the floor back to back. They should lean up against one another for support.

Each pair of participants needs a clipboard, pencil, and crayons or markers. Give one object to the partner in each pair who will be describing the object. *Make sure the partner who will be drawing cannot see the object.* Choose small enough objects that one participant can hold it without the other participant seeing it. The goal of the game is for the participant holding the object to describe the object to the person holding the clipboard so that they can draw it on the paper.

Say:

- You will have 5 minutes to describe your object to your partner. The goal is for your partner to draw your object based *only* on the description you give.
- You can use words to tell your partner about the object, like its size, shape, color, and texture, but you cannot say what it is.
- For example, if I was describing a shoe to my partner, I could say, "It is about 6" wide and 10" long. It is sort of an oval shape. It has six long, skinny, horizontal lines that go across it. The bottom inch is black and the rest of it is red."
- Don't describe its function or the way it is used. For example: I could not say, "It has laces and a sole. It is what you walk on."

- After the 5 minutes is up, partners compare the drawing with the object.
- Once everyone is in place, we will start together when I say "Go!"

Once participants are in place, set a timer for 5 minutes and say:
- Go!

After 5 minutes—whether participants have a clear drawing or not—call "time."

Participants should stop and compare what they drew with the object. Ask pairs to switch roles—the one who drew now describes; the one who described now draws. Give the describer a new object, again without letting the one drawing see it.

When done, use these questions to facilitate a conversation.
- How close did your drawing come to the object you were given?
- What made it hard to accomplish this task?

Hopefully participants will say something about how they could not see the object or how they had a hard time not just saying what it was.

Ask:
- What would have made it easier?

Hopefully participants will say something about how it would have been easier if their partner did a better job describing it or if they were able to just look at it themselves.

Discuss:
- In our first session together we talked about being God's creation. Today's session will continue to build on what we explained was the *Imago Dei*, or the image of God. Just like it was hard for you to draw an accurate image of your object, it is hard to explain how humans were made in the image of God. Why do you think it might be hard to explain?
- Since we do not have the ability to look directly at God, all we can do is read what the Bible says and consider it with our minds and hearts. We can describe God with words, but they never give a total picture of God. For example, we can say that God is loving, so human beings have the capacity to love.
- The most amazing thing about God for Christians is that God was willing to take on human form, to put on our flesh, and become like us. God came as Jesus. This means that though we cannot possibly picture God completely, we can trust that God understands what it is like to be human.
- Though we cannot draw a picture of God, the image of God in each of us is still there.

GRAPPLE

NOTES

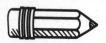

 45 minutes

Each Small-Group Leader will need to turn to this page (86) in their *Leader Guides* to facilitate this activity.

Info for Facilitators and Small-Group Leaders:

- Participants and adults alike have embedded understandings of the human body.
- Participants are bombarded with unrealistic images of the human body. They are fed a diet of digitally enhanced pictures to which they compare their own growing bodies.
- According to Brown University:
- Body image is a widespread preoccupation. In one study of college participants, 74.4% of the normal-weight women stated that they thought about their weight or appearance "all the time" or "frequently." But the women weren't alone; the study also found that 46% of the normal-weight men surveyed responded the same way.
- Letting go of poor body image requires replacing it with a foundation built upon scripture and a deeper understanding that we are made in the image of God. This session builds upon the first session, You Are GOD'S CREATION.

On a sheet of easel paper write the question: *Made in the Image of God?* Post this where all can see.

Say:
- At your tables you will find an assortment of magazines.
- You have probably seen these in the checkout line at the grocery store.
- Take a moment to look through one or more of the magazines.
- We are going to make a collage of advertisements featuring people we find attractive or interesting.
- Search for an advertisement featuring someone who stimulates your interest. Look for something that draws you in.

- When you have found a suitable picture, cut it out or tear it out of the magazine and glue it onto the paper with the question: *Made in the image of God?*
- Everyone should find an advertisement with someone (or several people) in it and add it to the collage.

Once everyone has had a chance to find an image, invite participants to return to their seats at their tables for discussion.

Say:
- Find someone beside you and quickly list three things you observe about the images on the easel paper. Ready? GO!

Give pairs about a minute to discuss.

Continue:
- Let each pair at your table share with those at your table one thing that they observed.

Allow time for pairs to share at their table, then ask each table to report back to the group a few of the observations of those at their table. You can record these for everyone to see on another sheet of easel paper or on a whiteboard or chalkboard.

Ask:
- Why do you think companies use images of people in their advertisements?

Eventually, if the discussion has not yet already naturally unfolded toward attraction, guide participants to ponder what natural human thought pattern could be at work. The goal of many advertisements is the exploitation of basic human desires. The advertising companies are using our desires to sell us products, many times products unrelated to the pictures shown.

Ask questions such as:
- Why is the woman on the tractor dressed that way?
- What is this ad selling? Does the picture relate to the product?

For the next part of the session, the Facilitator writes on the easel paper. You might want to prepare this part of the session before the session begins:
- Begin by dividing the easel paper lengthwise with a line down the middle. Then draw a horizontal line so that the easel paper looks like a capital *T*. This is called a *T-chart*.
- Above the horizontal line on the right side of the paper you will eventually add a title. For now, leave this side blank.
- On the left hand side above the horizontal line write the title *PICTURES*.

Ask:
- According to the pictures in our collage, what is the definition of an attractive human body?
- What do they convey about what society finds desirable?
- What are some adjectives that would describe what is found in these advertisements?

Record participants' answers on the left side of the paper.

Now title the right side of the paper with the word *FAITH.*

Discuss:
- Think about what you have already learned during our time together. Let's talk about who or what is accepted by God. How might we imagine God would define beauty?
- What does the Bible say is "good?"
- In our first sessions, we read a passage in Genesis that spoke of God's declaration about all of creation. There are two other places where the Bible mentions how humanity was created in God's image. Genesis 5 begins by referring back to the creation story. It states, "God created humanity, he made them to resemble God and created them male and female. He blessed them and called them humanity on the day they were created" (Genesis 5:1b-2, *CEB*). Similarly, after the story of the flood, speaking of the preciousness of human life, the passage states, "For in the divine image God made human beings" (Genesis 9:6b, *CEB*).
- Do we have photos of those "first human beings?"
- Who do we think is fully accepted by God?
- We know that God created us and called us good.
- In Christ, we have an example of the perfect image of God in human form.
- We also believe that by the power of God at work in our lives through the Holy Spirit, we can gradually look more and more like Christ, not physically, of course, but emotionally, mentally, and spiritually . . . perhaps even sexually. This is the journey of a lifetime.
- We know that we are loved and accepted by God, just the way we are, but God believes in us too much to leave us that way.[32] God works to help us be more Christ-like.
- In the New Testament book of Hebrews it states, "In the past, God spoke through the prophets to our ancestors in many times and many ways. In these final days, though, he spoke to us through a Son. God made his Son the heir of everything and created the world through him. The Son is the light of God's glory and the imprint of God's being. He maintains everything with his powerful message. After he carried out the cleansing of people from their sins, he sat down at the right side of the highest majesty" (Hebrews 1:1–3, *CEB*).
- In Colossians 1 we read about Jesus. It states, "The Son is the image of the invisible God, the one who is first over all creation" (Colossians 1:15, *CEB*).
- What do you think the phrase *imprint of God's being* means in the passage from Hebrews?
- When we use the standards of society to determine our value, we are sure to fall short. As Christians, we know that God's acceptance of us is not dependent upon our physical beauty or outward appearance. We know that God accepts us as we are and loves us unconditionally.

In Session 1 participants learned that in Genesis God declared humanity "very good." The clash between culture and faith is all too evident in this exercise. In future sessions the clash will continue to come up.

....

32 Adapted from the statement by Max Lucado, quoted by Presiding Bishop Michael Curry in his sermon at General Convention 2015.

Conclude the conversation by saying:
- Everyone move so that you can see the television or video screen.
- As you watch the Dove Real Beauty campaign clip think about how it fits into our session today. Notice how the model's appearance changes and how the computer editors create the image for the billboard. After the clip is over, I will ask each of you to tell the group something that you saw that was edited or changed.

Show the video clip of Dove's Evolution Campaign: https://www.youtube.com/watch?v=iYhCn0jf46U.

Say:
- Let's try something called "popcorn" feedback.
- We will take turns saying one thing that we noticed in the clip that we did not know before or that we found shocking. Then, we say, "Popcorn, *(name of participant.)*" This passes it on to the next person.

Facilitate this discussion, then continue:
- Why is it important to see the difference between our culture's definition of beauty and the Bible's description of humanity?
- In what ways is physical beauty connected to sexuality? In our *culture*, how are they connected? In our *faith*, how are they connected?
- A 2006 study published in the journal of *Psychology of Men and Masculinity* showed that not only did watching prime-time television and music videos appear to make men more uncomfortable with themselves, but that the discomfort led to sexual problems and risky behaviors. "People see the same images over and over and start to believe it's a version of reality," says Deborah Schooler, one of the researchers. "If those bodies are real and that's possible, but you can't attain it, how can you not feel bad about your own body?"
- When we see these images from the media, we tend to receive our sense of beauty from the images in movies, magazines, and websites, instead of our faith.
- Remember that God has created each of us uniquely. You are a *Child of God*, a *beautiful creation.*
- Remember that in Christ, through the power of the Holy Spirit, you are accepted by God.
- Growing up in the midst of these conflicting messages between our faith and culture can be difficult. It can be hard to remember the positive messages that we get from our faith.
- Thinking about the messages that we get in society, as people of faith, what can we do?
- How can we listen to the messages in our faith?
- Yes, we can come to church. Yes, we can spend time with friends and family who appreciate our whole selves. We can read the Bible and pray.

GUIDE

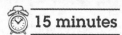 15 minutes

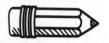

The Facilitator leads this portion of the session.

Pass out small pieces of paper to each participant. Explain:

- Each of you will be writing a question for the Question Box, as you will be asked to do in every session. This is a great place to have your questions answered.
- Everyone needs to write a question. For example, you might ask about a word that you've heard but don't understand or a joke that you don't get. If you don't have a question of your own, think of a question that might be asked by someone your age.
- The Small-Group Leaders and the Facilitator will answer your questions at the beginning of the next session.

The Facilitator moves around the room with the Question Box to collect the questions.

After everyone has submitted a question, invite all participants (leaders and participants) to join in a large enough space where you can form a circle. After you have made the circle, invite everyone to move close enough to each other that they are touching shoulder to shoulder. Invite everyone to relax and take a deep breath. As they relax, they should naturally stop touching shoulders so closely, yet maintain an appropriate level of intimacy for this portion of the session.

Invite all in the circle to close their eyes for a few seconds and slow their breathing. Maintain this for about 30 seconds.

Say:
- When we watch television, read magazines, scroll through social media, and walk through the mall, advertisements overtake our senses.
- They consistently tell us how to define beauty in an unhealthy way. They constantly make us feel like we have to look a certain way in order to be accepted by those around us.

- They set an unreachable standard.
- As we close our session today, I want to invite you to quietly reflect for a moment on this statement: God accepts us as we are and loves us unconditionally.

Let the group sit quietly for about one minute.

The Facilitator continues:
- Genesis tells us, "God created humanity in God's own image, in the divine image God created them, male and female God created them," (Genesis 1:27, *CEB*). You are each made in the likeness of God.
- Sometimes, when we have accepted a flawed way of thinking, the first step to correcting it is to hear the truth out loud. Today we learned our culture's definition of beauty is flawed, but God accepts us as we are and works in us to make us more like Christ, the perfect example of God's image in human form.

Look around the circle. Select one participant to be the first to offer the statement of affirmation found below. The person should be someone you are confident can set the group in the right direction. Say to that person:
- *(Name of participant)*, I invite you to start us off in this next activity. I'd like you to choose someone in the group. Say to that person, "*(Name)*, you are accepted by God."

Then say to the entire group:
- The person to whom this is said will select someone else in the group and repeat the statement for that new person.
- We will continue until everyone in the group—both leaders and participants—has been affirmed.

Be sure everyone gets a chance to speak *and to be affirmed*.

GO

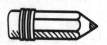

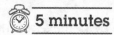 5 minutes

The Facilitator leads this portion of the session.

Sending participants and leaders back into their daily lives is the final step in the session. This section is meant to be simple and quick.

Say:

- Leaving this time together requires a shift. This is a safe place. This is a place where we are learning and growing together. Outside of this place are our homes, schools, families, friends, and many other social circles.
- What I want to leave you with at the end of each session is that no matter where you are in the world, no matter who you are with, God is with you on your journey.
- Let us close with prayer:

  Leader: The Lord be with you.
  Participants: And also with you.
  Leader: Let us pray.

  Creator God, giver of the divine image, hold us tightly within your arms of love so that even when we do not feel beautiful by the standards of the world, we are able to claim your image imprinted on us, in the name of God our life-giver, Jesus our life-redeemer, and Holy Spirit our life-perfecter. *Amen.*

AFTER·THE·SESSION
DEBRIEF

For Facilitator and Small-Group Leaders Only

Please see the full material found in Session 1, page 57.

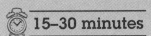 15–30 minutes

NOTES

SESSION 4

YOU ARE
RELATIONAL (PART 1)

No one has greater love than this, to lay down one's life for
one's friends.

—John 15:13, *NRSV*

As children of God, we are relational people—people who are called to love and serve one another. The greatest commandment sets the stage for our intentional mission of loving others. But why are relationships so important in the Christian life. Our relationships are the proving ground of life. Our friendships, our acquaintances, and our intimate lifelong bonds provide the ground on which we work to become more Christ-like. As relational people, we grow up into the full stature of Christ in our relationships—learning to love one another as Christ loved us and to "manifest the grace of God, the gifts of the Spirit, and holiness of life."[33]

Middle-schoolers are continuing the journey of friendships—building them, nurturing them, growing and learning from them. They are becoming more independent in their choices of friends and may begin to make "unexpected"

friendships as their need for independence grows. These two sessions on relationships—You are RELATIONAL (Part 1) and You are RELATIONAL (Part 2)—offer participants biblical examples of friendship that demonstrate the holiness of friendship. Participants continue to learn about and grow in love primarily through friendships. They bear witness to the uncontained love of God through Christ in the relationships that they are forming. Some of this powerful learning will happen *in this session* as the participants form lasting bonds. We are on holy ground.

As you move through these sessions be mindful of the participants. Notice if anyone is feeling anxious or uncomfortable.

---

33 *Liturgical Resources 1: I Will Bless You and You Will Be a Blessing,* Supplemental Materials (NY: Church Publishing, 2005), 25. Standing Commission of Liturgy and Music, 25.

OBJECTIVES

❑ Participants will know the differences and similarities of friendship, love, and infatuation.
❑ Participants will identify qualities of loyalty, respect, mutuality, and commitment in Bible passages.

NOTES

_____

_____

_____

_____

_____

_____

_____

_____

❏ Participants will analyze their own relationships to determine if they display the same qualities.

❏ Participants will discover that love, infatuation, and friendship are not independent from one another.

❏ Participants will discover that relationships are complex because human beings are complex.

SUPPLIES

❏ pencils or pens (1 per participant)

❏ highlighter (1 per participant)

❏ *These Are Our Bodies Participant Books* (1 per participant)

❏ *These Are Our Bodies Leader Guide* (1 for the Facilitator and 1 for each Small-Group Leader)

❏ HOPE poster[34] (See pp. 13–14.)

❏ easel paper and markers

❏ scrap pieces of colored paper for the Question Box (3" x 5")

----

34 The authors have done their best, without success, to track down the original source of the HOPE acronym. No copyright infringement is intended. If notified, they will gladly credit the original author in future editions of *These Are Our Bodies*.

❏ Question Box (See directions, pp. 14–17.)

❏ nametags

❏ 2 copies of the *Love Strips* found on pages 213–214 in the Appendix, cut apart, 1 for each team in today's GAME

❏ 2 containers to hold the *Love Strips*, 1 for each team in today's GAME

❏ *optional:* music player and quiet, reflective music for journaling (If you use a phone to play music, bring an external speaker. If you forget your speaker, place the phone in a plastic cup—a Solo cup is perfect. The cup amplifies the sound. Try it—it works!)

PREPARATION

❏ Gather needed supplies. Set up the room for the session. Arrange furniture and materials so that they are readily available and designed for discussion.

❏ If you are using music, test the device and the sound projection.

❏ Read through the background information about the scripture passages, found in GRAPPLE, below.

GATHER

NOTES

_____
_____
_____
_____
_____
_____
_____
_____
_____
_____
_____
_____
_____
_____
_____
_____
_____
_____
_____
_____
_____
_____
_____

 20 minutes

As participants enter, have them put on their nametags, pick up their *Participant Books,* and select a pencil or pen.

HOPE Poster

Gain participants' attention and say:
- Welcome everyone. As we begin today, *(name of participant)* is going to lead us in today's GATHER.
- Who would like to lead us next week?

Make a note of the volunteer for next week.

Participant says:
- Let's look together at our HOPE poster.
- Stand and join me as we read together:

  Honesty: We commit to sharing what we really think.
  Openness: We commit to being open to what others say, both our group members and our leaders, and most of all to God.
  Privacy: We commit to keeping what is said and done here within this space.
  Enthusiasm: We commit to laughter, fun, and a sense of wonder.

Prayer

Lead participants in this prayer:
> O Lord, you have taught us that without love whatever we do is worth nothing: Send your Holy Spirit and pour into our hearts your greatest gift, which is love, the true bond of peace and of all virtue, without which whoever lives is accounted dead before

you. Grant this for the sake of your only Son Jesus Christ, who lives and reigns with you and the Holy Spirit, one God, now and forever. *Amen*.[35]

The Question Box

Note: Be sure you have read the full explanation of the Question Box found on pages 14–17 of the Introduction. Please see the full material found in Session 3, page 83.

Guidelines for answering questions:

- Think about the time that it will take to answer the questions. An average of 60–90 seconds per question is a reasonable guideline. Answering questions for a group of 6–8 participants will take 8–12 minutes.
- Adjust the amount of time that you allow based on your group.
- Do not over-explain. Keep it moving!
- Go down the question list one by one and answer each question. The Small-Group Leaders and the Facilitator will have already decided how to answer each question and who will answer the question at the end of last session.
- Remember to answer the questions clearly and concisely. You are aiming for a 45–60 second answer.
- Don't belabor the answers. You will want to spend as much time on the session as you can.

When all the questions have been answered, say:
- You all asked great questions.
- Remember that you will have an opportunity to write a question for the Question Box at the end of this session.

---

35 Book of Common Prayer, Seventh Sunday after the Epiphany, page 216.

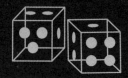

GAME

Act It Out

 20 minutes

For each session's Game, consider moving the group to an alternative location—another area of the same room, another room, a space outdoors, etc. Young people benefit from movement and a change of seating.

Act It Out introduces 1 Corinthians 13:4–7 as a way to describe Christian love. Here are these verses, from the *Common English Bible*:

> [4]Love is patient, love is kind, it isn't jealous, it doesn't brag, it isn't arrogant,
> [5]it isn't rude, it doesn't seek its own advantage, it isn't irritable, it doesn't keep a record of complaints,
> [6]it isn't happy with injustice, but it is happy with the truth.
> [7]Love puts up with all things, trusts in all things, hopes for all things, endures all things.

This session and the next will touch on three aspects of relationships: *love, infatuation,* and *friendship*. Today's GAME introduces the first of these—*love*.

Say:

- In the first letter of Paul to the church at Corinth, also called 1 Corinthians, there is a famous set of verses about love.
- You may have even memorized part of it, seen it on a greeting card, or read it on a piece of wall art.
- To help us think through these verses, you are going to be divided up into two teams.

Divide participants into two teams of equal number by counting off: A, B, A, B, A, B, etc. **Note:** If you do not have enough participants to create teams, you can make it an individual challenge. Have individual participants take turns acting out the saying. Remaining participants try to guess what the participant is acting out. After the group guesses correctly, another participant draws from the container and acts out what is on the strip.

Say:

- First, you have 10 seconds to come up with a team name. The team name should have something to do with love. Ready . . . GO!

Count down from 10 out loud for all to hear.

Ask:

- What are your team names?

Say:

- Each team will need a timekeeper who will keep time for the other team.
- Who will keep time for *(first team name)*?
- Who will keep time for *(second team name)*?

On easel paper, create a T-chart for keeping score with the two team names at the top. Have a container ready with strips of paper that have phrases from the Corinthians passage written on them. Give each small group a container containing the *Love Strips* prepared before the session.

Continue:

- The goal of this game is to score the most points as a team. It is kind of like charades with a twist. Either individually or in pairs, you will draw a *Love Strip* from your team's container. On it is a specific part of these verses from 1 Corinthians 13 that describes love.
- It is your job to act out the words on the strip of paper. For example, if it says, "Love is happy with the truth," you might act out someone telling the truth. Maybe one person is the friend and the other person is coming clean about something they did wrong. Or maybe it is someone speaking up for what is true and just. You are allowed to speak words, but they cannot be the words from the verses.
- You will have 1 minute to act out your phrase for your team to guess.
- If you know the answer, just call it out.
- Small-Group Leaders will help keep the game moving by keeping time.
- These are the phrases that you will be acting out:
  ○ Love is patient
  ○ Love is kind
  ○ Love is not jealous
  ○ Love does not brag
  ○ Love is not arrogant
  ○ Love is not rude
  ○ Love does not seek its own advantage
  ○ Love is not irritable
  ○ Love does not keep a record of complaints
  ○ Love is not happy with injustice
  ○ Love is happy with the truth
  ○ Love puts up with all things
  ○ Love trusts in all things

- ○ Love hopes for all things
- ○ Love endures all things
- I am going to read the phrases again one more time. Pay careful attention so you can guess well.

Reread the list above, then say:
- In your team, decide who will play first.

When groups are ready, say:
- Let's begin.
- Okay *(team name),* you are first. Draw a strip and act it out.
- The other team will time. Remember you have 1 minute to act out the phrase on the strip you draw.
- Ready, Set, GO.

When the turn is done, say:
- Well done!
- Now *(second team's name),* it is your turn. Who's first on the *(team name)*?

The first person on the other team draws a strip. The opposing team keeps time. If participants seem to need more time, add time to the game. The idea is to have fun while learning, so feel free to adjust as needed. Go back and forth between the two teams until they have acted out all or most of the verses.

When all of the strips are gone or the time limit is reached, pull the participants back, turn to page 31 in their *Participant Book,* and discuss:
- Think about the verses about love that you just acted out.
- Which of the verses were the most difficult to act out?
- Let's look at the verses again. Are there some of the verses that you have a hard time showing in your life?

Offer examples, if needed, to get the conversation going, like this:
- Look at the verse: "Love does not keep a record of complaints." How do we do with that one? Anyone good at complaining? It's a high standard. What other verses are difficult?

Continue:
- What happens when only one person in a relationship follows these verses and the other person does the opposite?

Conclude the Game section of today's session by saying:
- *Love* is one of the three words we are studying today.
- We also want to discuss *friendship* and *infatuation*.
- As we move into the GRAPPLE portion of our session, remember what Paul's letter described as love. See what you discover about a relationship between two men in the Old Testament book of 1 Samuel.

GRAPPLE

 45 minutes

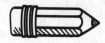

Have the two teams come together as one large group for this first part of GRAPPLE. This GRAPPLE has an introduction led by the Facilitator. Then participants move back into their teams to read scripture, discuss the passages, and complete questions in their *Participant Book*.

As you move into this section, hand a highlighter to each participant and visually check that everyone has their *Participant Book* and a pen or pencil. Check that all are on the correct page in their *Participant Book*.

Background on Jonathan and David

The story of Jonathan and David is one of friendship and love. David is well known for his defeat of Goliath when the king of the people was Saul. David was the youngest child of Jesse and was chosen to be the next King of Israel. This story occurs after the story of David and Goliath when David is likely a little bit older.

The main characters of the story are:
- King Saul, a good king who becomes cruel and jealous
- Jonathan, the son of King Saul and the prince of Israel
- Michal, the daughter of King Saul and wife of David
- David, the son of Jesse who lives in the palace with Saul and Jonathan

David was a shepherd and a loyal and brave young man. He even rescued one of his father's sheep from a lion and a bear. He was chosen by the prophet Samuel to be the next king. Normally, the king's son would inherit the throne. Although Jonathan was the prince, he was not chosen to follow his father as king. Once David was chosen, he was sent to live in the palace with King Saul and Jonathan. He became close to King Saul and Jonathan. Saul liked David, and he grew in favor with the king. Although Saul liked David, Saul often became angry and suspicious of David's loyalty. Over time, Jonathan and David became very close friends.

Participants in middle school have relationships on many different levels. The story of David and Jonathan is not only beautiful; it embodies a kind of relationship and love that is loyal, respectful, mutual, and committed.

The Facilitator begins today's GRAPPLE by saying:
- Make sure you have your *Participant Book*, a pen, and a highlighter
- Turn to page 30 to follow along with today's GRAPPLE.
- Today we are going to begin by reading about an interesting relationship in the Bible, the friendship of Jonathan and David.
- In your *Participant Books* you will find these stories as they have been recorded in the Old Testament. Turn in your *Participant Book* to page 37. When you have found the correct page, look up at me so I know we are ready to move on.
- Who has heard of King David before? What do you remember about him?

Participants will likely recall the story of David slaying Goliath or that of David and Bathsheba. Establish that this is the same David they may have heard about as a small child, but that David's life is one of the best-recorded lives in the entire Bible. Therefore, we know a great deal about his life from when he was young and killed Goliath to when he became King and ruled the people.

If participants do not remember much about David, read the story summary or retell the summary in your own words.

Ask group members and Small-Group Leaders to gather in their teams (use the same teams that you used for the GAME). You will want the two teams to spread out from each other, so the conversation and reading of scripture is not disturbing to the other team.

The Facilitator then says:
- You will be working in your *Participant Book* for this portion of the session with your Small-Group Leader. You will be in the same team that you were in for the GAME portion of the session.
- Follow along in your *Participant Books* as your Small-Group Leaders read the passages. Highlight or underline words or phrases that stand out to you. Think about the things that Jonathan and David did for each other that demonstrated their friendship.

Ask the Small-Group Leaders to each read a section of the scripture, printed here:

1 Samuel 18: 1–5 (*CEB*)
¹As soon as David had finished talking with Saul, Jonathan's life became bound up with David's life, and Jonathan loved David as much as himself. ²From that point forward, Saul kept David in his service and wouldn't allow him to return to his father's household. ³And Jonathan and David made a covenant together because Jonathan loved David as much as himself. ⁴Jonathan took off the robe he was wearing and gave it to David, along with his armor, as well as his sword, his bow, and his belt. ⁵David went out and was successful in every mission Saul sent him to do. So Saul placed him in charge of the soldiers, and this pleased all the troops as well as Saul's servants.

1 Samuel 20:1–42 (*CEB*)

¹David fled from the camps at Ramah. He came to Jonathan and asked, "What have I done? What is my crime? How have I wronged your father that he wants me dead?" ²Jonathan said to him, "No! You are not going to die! Listen: My father doesn't do anything big or small without telling me first. Why would my father hide this from me? It isn't true!" ³But David solemnly promised in response, "Your father knows full well that you like me. He probably said, 'Jonathan must not learn about this or he'll be upset.' But I promise you— on the Lord's life and yours!—that I am this close to death!" "What do you want me to do?" Jonathan said to David. "I'll do it." ⁵"Okay, listen," David answered Jonathan. "Tomorrow is the new moon, and I'm supposed to sit with the king at the feast. Instead, let me go and I'll hide in the field until nighttime. ⁶If your father takes note of my absence, tell him, 'David begged my permission to run down to his hometown Bethlehem, because there is an annual sacrifice there for his whole family.' ⁷If Saul says 'Fine,' then I, your servant, am safe. But if he loses his temper, then you'll know for certain that he intends to harm me. ⁸So be loyal to your servant, because you've brought your servant into a sacred covenant with you. If I'm guilty, then kill me yourself; just don't take me back to your father." ⁹"Enough!" Jonathan replied. "If I can determine for certain that my father intends to harm you, of course I'll tell you!" ¹⁰"Who will tell me if your father responds harshly?" David asked Jonathan. ¹¹"Come on," Jonathan said to David. "Let's go into the field." So both of them went out into the field. ¹²Then Jonathan told David, "I pledge by the Lord God of Israel that I will question my father by this time tomorrow or on the third day. If he seems favorable toward David, I will definitely send word and make sure you know. ¹³But if my father intends to harm you, then may the Lord deal harshly with me, Jonathan, and worse still if I don't tell you right away so that you can escape safely. May the Lord be with you as he once was with my father. ¹⁴If I remain alive, be loyal to me. But if I die, ¹⁵don't ever stop being loyal to my household. Once the Lord has eliminated all of David's enemies from the earth, ¹⁶if Jonathan's name is also eliminated, then the Lord will seek retribution from David!" ¹⁷So Jonathan again made a pledge to David because he loved David as much as himself.

¹⁸"Tomorrow is the festival of the new moon," Jonathan told David. "You will be missed because your seat will be empty. ¹⁹The day after tomorrow, go all the way to the spot where you hid on the day of the incident, and stay close to that mound. ²⁰On the third day I will shoot an arrow to the side of the mound as if aiming at a target. ²¹Then I'll send the servant boy, saying, 'Go retrieve the arrow.' If I yell to the boy, 'Hey! The arrow is on this side of you. Get it!' then you can come out because it will be safe for you. There won't be any trouble—I make a pledge on the Lord's life. ²²But if I yell to the young man, 'Hey! The arrow is past you,' then run for it, because the Lord has sent you away. ²³Either way, the Lord is witness between us forever regarding the promise we made to each other." ²⁴So David hid himself in the field. When the new moon came, the king sat at the feast to eat. ²⁵He took his customary seat by the wall. Jonathan sat opposite him while Abner sat beside Saul. David's seat was empty.

²⁶Saul didn't say anything that day because he thought, Perhaps David became unclean somehow. That must be it. ²⁷But on the next day, the second of the new moon, David's seat was still empty. Saul said to his son Jonathan, "Why hasn't Jesse's son come to the table, either yesterday or today?" ²⁸Jonathan answered Saul, "David begged my permission to go to

Bethlehem. 29He said, 'Please let me go because we have a family sacrifice there in town, and my brother has ordered me to be present. Please do me a favor and let me slip away so I can see my family.' That's why David hasn't been at the king's table."

30At that, Saul got angry at Jonathan. "You son of a stubborn, rebellious woman!" he said. "Do you think I don't know how you've allied yourself with Jesse's son? Shame on you and on the mother who birthed you! 31As long as Jesse's son lives on this earth, neither you nor your dynasty will be secure. Now have him brought to me because he's a dead man!" 32But Jonathan answered his father Saul, "Why should David be executed? What has he done?" 33At that, Saul threw his spear at Jonathan to strike him, and Jonathan realized that his father intended to kill David. 34Jonathan got up from the table in a rage. He didn't eat anything on the second day of the new moon because he was worried about David and because his father had humiliated him. 35In the morning, Jonathan went out to the field for the meeting with David, and a young servant boy went with him. 36He said to the boy, "Go quickly and retrieve the arrow that I shoot." So the boy ran off, and he shot an arrow beyond him. 37When the boy got to the spot where Jonathan shot the arrow, Jonathan yelled to him, "Isn't the arrow past you?" 38Jonathan yelled again to the boy, "Quick! Hurry up! Don't just stand there!" So Jonathan's servant boy gathered up the arrow and came back to his master. 39The boy had no idea what had happened; only Jonathan and David knew. 40Jonathan handed his weapons to the boy and told him, "Get going. Take these back to town."

41As soon as the boy was gone, David came out from behind the mound and fell down, face on the ground, bowing low three times. The friends kissed each other, and cried with each other, but David cried hardest. 42Then Jonathan said to David, "Go in peace because the two of us made a solemn pledge in the Lord's name when we said, 'The Lord is witness between us and between our descendants forever.'" Then David got up and left, but Jonathan went back to town.

Small-Group Leaders say to their teams:
• How many of you have heard this story of David's life before?

Small-Group Leaders let participants say whether this is familiar to them so that you can build on their prior knowledge or fill in the missing pieces.

Small-Group Leaders continue:
• We are looking at this particular story because it is about two young men who are in a relationship. Their relationship is on display in the story.
• In what ways did Jonathan show he was a trustworthy friend?

Participants' answers might mention these aspects:
• When David feared for his life at the hands of Jonathan's father Saul, Jonathan bravely remained loyal to David and the covenant between them.
• Jonathan did as David asked and warned David of Saul's intentions to kill him.
• Jonathan warned David and interceded for him so that he put his own life in danger, narrowly escaping death at the hand of his father, King Saul.

- Jonathan risked his life again when he traveled a great distance to see David in hiding, knowing that his father had spies watching every move.
- Jonathan did all of this even though he knew David would one day ascend the throne in his place.

Small-Group Leaders continue:
- What words or phrases in the passage specifically talk about how they care for each other?

Participants' answers might mention these words or phrases:
- "Jonathan's life became bound up with David's life, and Jonathan loved David as much as himself" (1 Samuel 18:1, *CEB*).
- "And Jonathan and David made a covenant together because Jonathan loved David as much as himself. Jonathan took off the robe he was wearing and gave it to David, along with his armor, as well as his sword, his bow, and his belt" (1 Samuel 18:3–4, *CEB*).
- "'What do you want me to do?' Jonathan said to David. 'I'll do it'" (1 Samuel 20:4, *CEB*).
- "If I remain alive, be loyal to me. But if I die, 15 don't ever stop being loyal to my household" (1 Samuel 20:14–15a, *CEB*).
- "So Jonathan again made a pledge to David because he loved David as much as himself" (1 Samuel 20:17, *CEB*).
- "As soon as the boy was gone, David came out from behind the mound and fell down, face on the ground, bowing low three times. The friends kissed each other, and cried with each other, but David cried hardest" (1 Samuel 20:41, *CEB*).

Small-Group Leaders continue:
- David trusted Jonathan with his own life, even when he knew Jonathan would have to betray his father.
- How does a friendship form that has that much trust?
- When you think about others trusting you, what behaviors of yours would inspire that trust?
- Think back to our verses from 1 Corinthians 13. What aspects of David and Jonathan's relationship demonstrate that kind of love?
- How did David and Jonathan both give and take in their relationship?
- David showed great loyalty to Saul and Jonathan. Even when presented with the opportunity to sneak up on Saul and kill him, David restrained himself. David remembered the covenant he made with his friend, recalling the words spoken between them.
- Jonathan says, "If I am still alive, show me the faithful love of the LORD; but if I die, never cut off your faithful love from my house, even if the LORD were to cut off every one of the enemies of David from the face of the earth." Thus Jonathan made a covenant with the house of David saying, "May the LORD seek out the enemies of David." Jonathan made David swear again by his love for him; for he loved him as he loved his own life" (1 Samuel 20:14–17, *NRSV*).
- What other qualities of true friendship did David and Jonathan exhibit?
- How did David and Jonathan show respect for each other?

Small-Group Leaders will facilitate this next part of the journaling in the *Participant Books*. The Facilitator may want to keep track of time and let the Small-Group Leaders know when to transition to the journaling. After the journaling time, everyone will rejoin the large group for GUIDE and GO.

Small-Group Leaders say:
- We are going to take a few minutes now to reflect on what we just read and discussed.
- In a moment, I want you to take your *Participant Book* and find a quiet place in the room by yourself.

Clearly define the parameters of where they can go and sit. You will want to call them back together after only a few minutes, so you may want to set the parameter for one specific room.

Small-Group Leader's say:
- In your *Participant Book*, turn to pages 41–42. There are five open-ended sentences for you to complete.
- When you are finished writing, you can signal that to me by closing your book and setting your pencil down.
- Take about 7 minutes now to write out your own endings to these sentences.

Note to Facilitator: Sometimes it is helpful to put on some reflective or fun music. Participants can feel intimidated by a super quiet space. Quiet does not have to mean silence; it can mean soft music playing. The Facilitator can start the music to set the stage for the participants to journal.

For your reference, here are the five open-ended questions; consider writing your own answers as a way of walking alongside the participants:
1. Friendship is . . .
2. True friendship feels like . . .
3. Being a friend means . . .
4. Friendships are sometimes hard when . . .
5. A friend . . . *(use verbs to complete this one—action words)*

The Facilitator calls participants and Small-Group Leaders back to the main area and gathers participants into one group. When all participants have finished with their sentences, transition directly into the GUIDE portion of today's session. Have participants keep their *Participant Books* with them. Have the Small-Group Leaders write their own responses to the five open-ended sentences and bring them to the GUIDE portion as well.

Facilitator says:
- It is time to come together for our GUIDE and GO.
- Bring your *Participant Books* with your five completed sentences.

GUIDE

⏰ 15 minutes

The Facilitator leads this portion of the session.

Pass out small pieces of paper to each participant. Explain:
- Each of you will be writing a question for the Question Box, as you will be asked to do in every session. This is a great place to have your questions answered.
- Everyone needs to write a question. For example, you might ask about a word that you've heard but don't understand or a joke that you don't get. If you don't have a question of your own, think of a question that might be asked by someone your age.
- The Small-Group Leaders and the Facilitator will answer your questions at the beginning of the next session.

The Facilitator moves around the room with the Question Box to collect the questions.

After everyone has submitted a question, invite all participants (leaders and participants) to join in a large enough space where you can form a circle. After you have made the circle, invite everyone to move close enough to each other that they are touching shoulder to shoulder. Invite everyone to relax and take a deep breath. As they relax, they should naturally stop touching shoulders so closely, yet maintain an appropriate level of intimacy for this portion of the session.

Invite all in the circle to close their eyes for a few seconds and slow their breathing. Maintain this for about 30 seconds.

Say:
- Thank you for writing a question for the Question Box. Your Small-Group Leaders and I will answer your questions at the beginning of the next session.
- Let all gather around together and bring your *Participant Books* with your five completed sentences.

Make sure that everyone, including the adults, has their open-ended sentence responses with them.

The Facilitator continues:
- Today we began our session with a game about some verses in 1 Corinthians. Those verses were about love. After the game we read about David (the young man who fought Goliath) and Jonathan (the son of King Saul).
- When we read about David and Jonathan, we saw a relationship that was COMPLEX, like we learned in Session 2. It was COMPLEX because human beings are COMPLEX.
- You have had some time to reflect on friendship. Hopefully you feel like friendship is something you are building with the participants in this room.
- In your *Participant Book* you finished some open-ended sentences. You finished sentences like, "Friendship is . . ." and "Being a friend means . . ." and "A friend . . ."
- In this circle, one of the opening statements we say is, "We commit to being open to what others say, both the group members and our Small-Group Leaders, and most of all to God."
- I invite you now to choose one of your open-ended sentences to read aloud to the group.

When everyone has had a turn, transition into the GO portion of the session. You may want to ask everyone to stand up, link arms, hold hands, or touch a shoulder. As the Facilitator, it is important to do what will benefit your group in the moment. Assess your group and help them close well.

GO

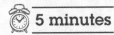 **5 minutes**

The Facilitator leads this portion of the session.

Sending participants and leaders back into their daily lives is the final step in the session. This section is meant to be simple and quick.

Say:

- Leaving this time together requires a shift. This is a safe place. This is a place where we are learning and growing together. Outside of this place are our homes, schools, families, friends, and many other social circles. Remember, no matter where you are in the world, no matter who you are with, God is with you on your journey.
- Let us close with prayer.

A Small-Group Leader reads:

Christ has no body now on earth but yours,
no hands but yours,
no feet but yours,
Yours are the eyes through which to look out
Christ's compassion to the world
Yours are the feet with which he is to go about
doing good;
Yours are the hands with which he is to bless those around you.[36]

Leader: The Lord be with you.
Participants: And also with you.
Leader: Let us pray.

....

36 *The British Friend*, volume 1, number 1, 1892, 1. Although this prayer is commonly attributed to Teresa of Avila, there is evidence that the prayer has two authors, Methodist Minister Mark Guy Pearse and Sarah Eliza Rowntree. It was published in its present form in 1892. For more information see http://livinginthemonasterywithoutwallsdotcom.wordpress.com/2013/02/04/christ-has-no-body-but-yours-teresa-of-avila/

Dear Lord
Give each of us open hearts to be the hands and feet of Christ in the world.
Open our eyes to see the people around us as your children.
Help us to recognize Christ in the faces near to us and those far away.
Create in us a spirit of love and peace.
In your son's name we pray.
Amen.

AFTER·THE·SESSION
DEBRIEF

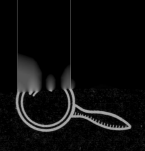

For Facilitator and Small-Group Leaders Only

Please see the full material found in Session 1, page 57.

 15–30 minutes

The time for this debrief will shift depending on the number and complexity of questions. Adjust the time for the debrief, if needed.

NOTES

YOU ARE RELATIONAL (PART 2)

Do not hesitate to love and to love deeply.[37]

—Henri Nouwen

37 Nouwen, Henri J. M., *The Inner Voice of Love: A Journey Through Anguish to Freedom*, (New York: Doubleday, 1996), 59–60.

OBJECTIVES

- ❏ Participants will know the differences and similarities of friendship, love, and infatuation.
- ❏ Participants will identify qualities of loyalty, respect, mutuality, and commitment in the Bible passages.
- ❏ Participants will analyze their own relationship to determine if they display the same qualities as those in the Bible passages.
- ❏ Participants will discover that love, infatuation, and friendship are not independent from one another.
- ❏ Participants will discover that relationships are complex because human beings are complex.

SUPPLIES

- ❏ pencils or pens (1 per participant)
- ❏ *These Are Our Bodies Participant Books* (1 per participant)
- ❏ *These Are Our Bodies Leader Guides* (1 for the Facilitator and 1 for each Small-Group Leader)

NOTES

- ❏ HOPE poster[38] (See pp. 13–14.)
- ❏ easel paper and markers
- ❏ scrap pieces of colored paper for the Question Box (3" x 5")
- ❏ Question Box (See directions, pp. 14–17.)
- ❏ nametags
- ❏ copies of the *Love Songs* handout (Appendix, pp. 215–217), 1 per participant

....

38 The authors have done their best, without success, to track down the original source of the HOPE acronym. No copyright infringement is intended. If notified, they will gladly credit the original author in future editions of *These Are Our Bodies*.

PREPARATION

- ❏ Gather needed supplies.
- ❏ Set up the room for the session. Arrange furniture and materials so that they are readily available and designed for discussion.
- ❏ Remember to read through the background information on the scripture passages for this session.

GATHER

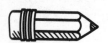

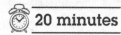 **20 minutes**

As participants enter, have them put on their nametags, pick up their *Participant Books,* and select a pencil or pen.

HOPE Poster

Gain participants' attention and say:
- Welcome everyone. As we begin today, *(name of participant)* is going to lead us in today's GATHER.
- Who would like to lead us next week?

Make a note of the volunteer for next week.

Participant says:
- Let's look together at our HOPE poster.
- Stand and join me as we read together:

Honesty: We commit to sharing what we really think.
Openness: We commit to being open to what others say, both our group members and our leaders, and most of all to God.
Privacy: We commit to keeping what is said and done here within this space.
Enthusiasm: We commit to laughter, fun, and a sense of wonder.

Prayer

Lead the opening prayer:

Holy God, one who took on flesh and lived as one of us,
dwell with us here and give us courage to learn, grow,
    and become more like you—
loving, kind, and full of grace—
through God our Creator, Christ our Redeemer,
and the Spirit our Sustainer. *Amen.*

The Question Box

Note: Be sure you have read the full explanation of the Question Box found on pages 14–17 of the Introduction. Please see the full material found in Session 3, page 83.

Guidelines for answering questions:

➤ Think about the time that it will take to answer the questions. An average of 60–90 seconds per question is a reasonable guideline. Answering questions for a group of 6–8 participants will take 8–12 minutes.

➤ Adjust the amount of time that you allow based on your group.

➤ Do not over-explain. Keep it moving!

➤ Go down the question list one by one and answer each question. The Small-Group Leaders and the Facilitator will have already decided how to answer each question and who will answer the question at the end of last session.

➤ Remember to answer the questions clearly and concisely. You are aiming for a 45–60 second answer.

➤ Don't belabor the answers. You will want to spend as much time on the session as you can.

When all the questions have been answered, say:

• You all asked great questions.

• Remember that you will have an opportunity to write a question for the Question Box at the end of this session.

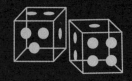

GAME

Change a Word, Ruin a Song

 20 minutes

This game does not require a great deal of movement, so it is possible to stay in the same room. If you want to add a movement break, build it into the GRAPPLE portion later in the session.

One of the goals of this game is humor. It is important to laugh together and develop a light-hearted atmosphere in the midst of such challenging topics. Both classic and modern love songs share one thing: *lyrics about love.* In this game, the goal is to ruin a classic or modern song by changing only one word.

Say:

- Last session we learned about relationships, focusing on both *love* and *friendship*. In this session, we want to build on those aspects of relationships but add in something new. In order to play this game, you need to know and understand a third term: *infatuation*.
- Infatuation happens quickly. It is an intense feeling that focuses on the positive aspects of someone.
- It can make us feel exhausted because we spend all of our time thinking about that one special person. It can take our attention away from other parts of our lives. Sometimes we are infatuated with someone because they take care of us. Sometimes relationships like this are full of jealousy or possessiveness.

Distribute the *Love Songs* handout (Appendix, pp. 215–217) and continue:

- Take a look at the handout. On it you will find a list of love songs—some old, some new. If you have access to technology and want to look up the lyrics to a few of the songs, that is acceptable. You can also ask the adults in the room to help you—they may know some of them by heart! Otherwise, work with just the titles.
- You're also free to add titles or lyrics from love songs that are popular right now.

- You will have 8 minutes to *ruin* as many love songs as possible by changing only *one* word in each title. As you do so, think about the new term: *infatuation*.
- Sometimes we focus on the wrong things with infatuation. For example, we can focus only on how *we* feel, or we may only be interested in how the relationship gives us what *we* want.
- Let's see if we can see how infatuation seems a little silly next to "love."
- So, how would love songs sound if they were all actually about infatuation? Here is an example of what I mean: Take the love song "All You Need is Love," by the Beatles. By changing the word "love" to the word "me," now the song is about infatuation.

At this point, be bold! Sing it for them!:
- "All you need is me. All you need is me! All you need is me, me. I am all you need."

Set the timer for 8 minutes.

Say:
- When the time is up, we will share them with each other. Ready, set, GO!

After 8 minutes is up, gather participants to share their "ruined" love songs.

GRAPPLE

NOTES

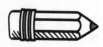

_____
_____
_____
_____
_____
_____
_____
_____
_____
_____
_____
_____
_____
_____
_____
_____
_____
_____
_____
_____
_____
_____
_____
_____
_____
_____

 45 minutes

Invite Small-Group Leaders to turn to pages 218–219 in the Appendix. There they will find the Situations to be discussed in their small groups. These situations are also found in the *Participant Book* on pages 49–51.

Say:
- Today we explore the story of Ruth, who became the great-grandmother of Jesus. It is also the story of a special friendship between Naomi and Ruth.
- Ruth's story is told in the book of Ruth in the Old Testament.

Write on the easel paper this list of people:
- Judah—a man from Bethlehem
- Naomi—wife to Judah, mother to two sons
- Ruth—married to one of Ruth's sons
- Orpah—married to one of Ruth's sons

Say:
- There are four main people in this story.
- Judah was a man from Bethlehem.
- Naomi was wife to Judah and the mother of two sons.
- Ruth was married to one of Naomi's sons.
- Orpah was married to another of Naomi's sons.

Either read this summary of the first part of the story of Ruth or tell it in your own words:
- During the time when judges ruled in Israel, there was a famine in the land. Judah and his wife Naomi decided to travel to a nearby country called Moab. They took their two sons with them to live in Moab hoping that there would be food and land to farm.
- When the sons became adults they married two Moab women. One was named Orpah and the other Ruth. Naomi's husband, Judah, died leaving Naomi alone with her two sons and their two wives. In that culture the sons would be responsible for taking care of their own wives. It was important for women to be married because that relationship kept women safe and protected. When a woman's husband died, her husband's family would take care

of her and her children as a way to honor the man who had died. When Judah died, this was very difficult for Naomi, because all she had were her two sons and their wives. Naomi stayed in Moab with her two sons and their wives.

- After about 10 years, Naomi's two sons both died, leaving Orpah and Ruth without husbands to care for them. Naomi had lost her husband and her two sons; she felt very alone.
- Naomi wanted leave the country of Moab to go back to Bethlehem because she had heard that there was more food in Bethlehem. Ruth was concerned for her two daughters-in-law, who no longer had husbands. Orpah and Ruth didn't know what to do either. They wondered if they should they stay with Naomi or go back to their own families.

Say:

- Now we are going to pick up the next part of the story and read the story from the Bible to find out what happened next to Naomi and Ruth.
- For the story of Ruth and Naomi, I want you to find a partner.
- You and your partner will read the story together. You can find a spot to sit together and take turns reading the verses.
- You will find these verses in your *Participant Books* on pages 45–46. I will walk around to answer questions if you have them.
- After you read the passage, answer the questions in your *Participant Book* (pp. 47–48) together with your partner. When everyone has finished, we will come back together as a group and share.

Make sure every person finds a partner. Remind participants to answer the questions after they have read the story. As they read, walk around and ensure that participants are making progress toward reading and answering questions.

Here is the passage participants will be reading (Ruth 1:8–17), as found in the *Participant Book*:

8Naomi said to her two daughters-in-law, "Go back each of you to your mother's house. May the Lord deal kindly with you, as you have dealt with the dead and with me. 9The Lord grant that you may find security, each of you in the house of your husband." Ruth and Orpah were both very sad and they cried.

10They said to her, "No, we will return with you to your people." 11Naomi replied, "Turn back, my daughters, why will you go with me? Do I still have sons in my womb that they may become your husbands? 12Turn back, my daughters, go your way, for I am too old to have a husband. Even if I thought there was hope for me, even if I should have a husband tonight and bear sons, 13would you then wait until they were grown? Would you then refrain from marrying? No, my daughters, it has been far more bitter for me than for you, because the hand of the Lord has turned against me." 14Then they wept aloud again.
Orpah kissed her mother-in-law, but Ruth clung to her.

15So she said, "See, your sister-in-law has gone back to her people and to her gods; return after your sister-in-law." 16But Ruth said, "Do not press me to leave you or to turn back from following you! Where you go, I will go; Where you lodge, I will lodge; your people shall be my people, and your God my God. 17Where you die, I will die—there will I be buried. May the Lord do thus and so to me, and more as well, if even death parts me from you!" When Naomi saw that Ruth was determined to stay with her and travel back to the land of Judah, she didn't argue with Ruth anymore.

Once participants are finished, gather them back together to discuss what they found:

- Now that everyone has finished, let's come back together and have a conversation about the story of Ruth.
- Describe Naomi and Ruth's relationship. Was it love? infatuation? friendship? Explain your choice(s) based on the passage.
- How do you think Ruth felt when she was faced with the decision of going home or staying with Naomi?
- How do you think Naomi felt when Ruth said she would stay with her?
- Did Ruth and Naomi respect one another? Give evidence for your answer.
- Were Ruth and Naomi equals? In other words, did their relationship have equality?
- The definition of "love" is not simple. The scriptures record the relationship between Ruth and Naomi as one that is complex. Just as we learned that we are complex and that David and Jonathan are complex, so are most of the relationships in the Bible—and in real life.
- We are going to back into our pairs from the last activity.
- On pages 49–51 of your *Participant Books* you will find some real-life complex relationships. Now that we have discussed love, friendship, and infatuation, take 7–10 minutes to consider some specific situations. With your partner, analyze these situations. In each case, your job is to determine whether the relationship is one of love, friendship, or infatuation.
- It is not important that you decide on the "correct" or "right" answer, but that you think through the relationship for yourself.

Have pairs spread out across the room and work through the *Situations* independently. Set a timer so that after 7–10 minutes pairs can come back together to form one large group.

The Facilitator and Small-Group Leaders walk around the room, helping participants stay on task.

When time is up, bring the participants back together for the GUIDE portion of the session.

GUIDE

⏰ 15 minutes

The Facilitator leads this portion of the session.

Pass out small pieces of paper to each participant. Explain:
- Each of you will be writing a question for the Question Box, as you will be asked to do in every session. This is a great place to have your questions answered.
- Everyone needs to write a question. For example, you might ask about a word that you've heard but don't understand or a joke that you don't get. If you don't have a question of your own, think of a question that might be asked by someone your age.
- The Small-Group Leaders and the Facilitator will answer your questions at the beginning of the next session.

The Facilitator moves around the room with the Question Box to collect the questions.

After everyone has submitted a question, invite all participants (leaders and participants) to join in a large enough space where you can form a circle.

Say:
- Deciding whether you are in love, in a healthy friendship, infatuated with someone, or a combination of the three requires you to first know the difference between the three. Though we have read about relationships and talked about relationships, deciding what kind of relationships *you* are in requires both self-awareness and the help of others.
- You don't have to decide if you are in love on your own. You don't have to decide if it is infatuation on your own. You don't have to decide if a friendship is healthy on your own. Talk about your relationships with others who can be honest and open with you. Talk about it with your parents.

- We have spent a lot of time together talking and learning. I want for us to consider making a promise to each other as we close. You can fill in the blank however you think. See what you think of this promise: *I will try to be the kind of friend that is_____.*
- When you are ready, complete the statement: *I will try to be the kind of friend that is ____.*

When everyone has had a turn, proceed to the GO portion of the session.

GO

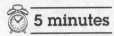 **5 minutes**

The Facilitator leads this portion of the session.

Sending participants and leaders back into their daily lives is the final step in the session. This section is meant to be simple and quick.

Say:

- Leaving this time together requires a shift. This is a safe place. This is a place where we are learning and growing together. Outside of this place are our homes, schools, families, friends, and many other social circles. Remember, no matter where you are in the world, no matter who you are with, God is with you on your journey.
- Let us close with prayer.

Leader: The Lord be with you.
Participants: And also with you.
Leader: Let us pray.

Gracious and Loving God,
you have blessed us with the gift of friends and family.
We thank you for the love that enfolds and the freedom to be ourselves.
 We thank you for those who know the love of friendship,
 who are patient in listening,
 who sit with us when we cry,
 who comfort us in pain,
 who celebrate with us in joy,
 who laugh with us delight,
 who remind us that we are God's children.
Bless our friends with faith, hope, and love.
Amen.

AFTER · THE · SESSION
DEBRIEF

For Facilitator and Small-Group Leaders Only

Please see the full material found in Session 1, page 57.

 15–30 minutes

The time for this debrief will shift depending on the number and complexity of questions. Adjust the time for the debrief, if needed.

NOTES

_____
_____
_____
_____
_____
_____
_____
_____
_____
_____
_____
_____
_____
_____
_____
_____
_____

SESSION 6

YOU ARE RESPONSIBLE

Sexuality is a gift from God—free and unearned. As with any gift from God, sexuality needs to be wrapped in good stewardship.

As we look at our freedom, we need also to look at our responsibility, which is more complex in Christ than our forebears could have imagined. We are responsible not only for our genital sexual activity, but for all the creativity that is an essential part of our humanity. We are accountable not only for acting in a morally responsible way, but for working out the meaning of redemption in our relationships with each other.[39]

....

39 Education for Mission & Ministry Unit. *Sexuality: A Divine Gift* (New York: Domestic and Foreign Missionary Society, 1987), 4.

Therefore, as a prisoner for the Lord, I encourage you to live as people worthy of the call you received from God. Conduct yourselves with all humility, gentleness, and patience. Accept each other with love, and make an effort to preserve the unity of the Spirit with the peace that ties you together.

—Ephesians 4:1–3, *NRSV*

OBJECTIVES

- ❑ Participants explore the metaphor of sex as fire.
- ❑ Participants discuss the commonalities of fire and sexuality.

- ❑ Participants identify ways that sexuality is a powerful, beautiful thing that needs to be wrapped in good stewardship.[40]
- ❑ Participants discuss how fire is good or bad and then transfer that insight into ways that sexuality can be a good thing or bad thing.
- ❑ Participants expand the metaphor of fire, to include sexuality and being to see that sexuality (like fire) is not good or bad, it is a gift. So much depends on how it is used.

40 "Sexuality is a gift from God. Although we sometimes identify sexuality with sexual activity and thus see sexuality as occupying a small isolated portion of our total living and being, we are foolish to deny our functioning as sexual beings. Through an understanding of the full range of love as described by C.S. Lewis (*agape, eros, store, filia*—divine love, passion, affection, and friendship, respectively) we understand the place of sexual activity and the source of sexual energy, which permeates our entire life" (*Sexuality: A Divine Gift,* 4).

NOTES

SUPPLIES

- ❏ pencils or pens (1 per participant)
- ❏ *These Are Our Bodies Participant Book* (1 per participant)
- ❏ *These Are Our Bodies Leader Guide* (1 for the Facilitator and 1 for each Small-Group Leader)
- ❏ HOPE poster[41] (See pp. 13–14.)
- ❏ easel paper and markers
- ❏ candles of different sizes and widths (5–7 candles)
- ❏ candle sticks or holders, if needed
- ❏ matches
- ❏ Post-it Notes® (1 *green* and 1 *yellow* per participant)
- ❏ scrap pieces of colored paper for the Question Box (3" x 5")
- ❏ Question Box (See directions, pp. 14–17.)
- ❏ nametags

....

41 The authors have done their best, without success, to track down the original source of the HOPE acronym. No copyright infringement is intended. If notified, they will gladly credit the original author in future editions of *These Are Our Bodies*.

PREPARATION

- ❏ Gather needed supplies.
- ❏ Set up the room for the session. Arrange furniture and materials so that they are readily available and designed for discussion.
- ❏ Before participants arrive, place the candles on the floor or on a table in the middle of the room and light them. The idea is to have fire in the room that seems to be unattended. You want to make some of the Small-Group Leaders or participants nervous about the lit candles.
- ❏ Write the prompts on the easel paper for the Poster Writing (see page XX).
- ❏ On easel paper, draw a T-chart. Title the left column *Fire is Good* and the right column *Fire is Bad.*

GATHER

NOTES

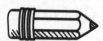

―――――――――――
―――――――――――
―――――――――――
―――――――――――
―――――――――――
―――――――――――
―――――――――――
―――――――――――
―――――――――――
―――――――――――
―――――――――――
―――――――――――
―――――――――――
―――――――――――
―――――――――――
―――――――――――
―――――――――――
―――――――――――
―――――――――――
―――――――――――
―――――――――――
―――――――――――
―――――――――――
―――――――――――

 5 minutes

As participants enter, have them put on their nametags, pick up their *Participant Books,* and select a pencil or pen.

HOPE Poster

Gain participants' attention and say:
- Welcome everyone. As we begin today, *(name of participant)* is going to lead us in today's GATHER.
- Who would like to lead us next week?

Make a note of the volunteer for next week.

Participant says:
- Let's look together at our HOPE poster.
- Stand and join me as we read together:

Honesty: We commit to sharing what we really think.
Openness: We commit to being open to what others say, both our group members and our leaders, and most of all to God.
Privacy: We commit to keeping what is said and done here within this space.
Enthusiasm: We commit to laughter, fun, and a sense of wonder.

Prayer

Holy God, one who took on flesh and lived as one of us,
dwell with us here and give us courage to learn, grow,
    and become more like you—
loving, kind, and full of grace—
through God our Creator, Christ our Redeemer,
and the Spirit our Sustainer. *Amen.*

The Question Box

Note: Be sure you have read the full explanation of the Question Box found on pages 14–17 of the Introduction. Please see the full material found in Session 3, page 83.

Guidelines for answering questions:

> ➤ Think about the time that it will take to answer the questions. An average of 60–90 seconds per question is a reasonable guideline. Answering questions for a group of 6–8 participants will take 8–12 minutes.
> ➤ Adjust the amount of time that you allow based on your group.
> ➤ Do not over-explain. Keep it moving!
> ➤ Go down the question list one by one and answer each question. The Small-Group Leaders and the Facilitator will have already decided how to answer each question and who will answer the question at the end of last session.
> ➤ Remember to answer the questions clearly and concisely. You are aiming for a 45–60 second answer.
> ➤ Don't belabor the answers. You will want to spend as much time on the session as you can.

When all the questions have been answered, say:
- You all asked great questions.
- Remember that you will have an opportunity to write a question for the Question Box at the end of this session.

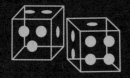

GAME

Poster-Writing

 15 minutes

Write the following prompts on *five* pieces of easel paper poster board (1 prompt per sheet). Write the letters 2"–3" high so the words can be read from anywhere in the room. Post these papers around the room at a height easily accessible to all:

- Gifts are . . .
- Love is . . .
- Risk-taking is . . .
- Being safe is . . .
- Responsibility is . . .

As participants enter the room, say:

- Select a marker or two.
- Walk around the room and write three or four words under each prompt that you think completes the sentence.

After all participants have finished writing on the papers, regather in the center of the room where the candles are lit. Have participants sit as close as they can to the candles. Some middle-schoolers may begin to play with the fire; allow safe interaction with the candles. Having participants interested in the fire will be a way to introduce other concepts later in the lesson.

GRAPPLE

 45 minutes

Each Small-Group Leader will need to turn to this page (135) in their *Leader Guides* to facilitate this activity.

Display the T-chart prepared before the session. Give each participant one *green* and one *yellow* Post-it Note and a marker. Say:

- Let's think about fire for a few minutes. We are going to talk about whether fire is a good thing or a bad thing. You will use your *green* Post-it Note to indicate a *good* thing; you will use your *yellow* Post-it Note to indicate a *bad* thing.
- If you think fire is a *good* thing, write why fire is good on your *green* note. If you think fire is a bad thing, write why fire is bad on your *yellow* note. Then you will stick the note on which you've written to the paper in the proper column on the chart.
- This is your "vote."

Observe what happens. Does one side of the chart "win"? Most likely, participants will see that fire is neither completely good nor completely bad. They will, in fact, want to "vote" on both sides of the board . . . or place their note in the middle of the board.

Ask:

- Which side won?

Say:

- Let's look further into this idea of fire being either good or bad.

Divide participants into groups with two Small-Group Leaders assigned to each group. Ask groups to complete the first part of the activity You Are Responsible, found on pages 54–56 in their *Participant Books*.

For your reference, here are the questions:

- Is fire *all bad?* Is fire *all good?*
- In what ways is fire a gift?
- When fire is dangerous or risky, what can you do to limit the danger?

- If fire is neither completely bad nor good, how would we think about fire?
- What can we do to stay safe?

Small-Group Leaders lead the participants through the questions in the *Participant Book*. After 10 minutes, come back together and process as a large group.

The Facilitator continues in the large group.

Discuss:
- Let's think more about fire. We are going to write the responses on easel paper.
- In what ways can fire be *bad*?

Allow time for brainstorming, recording answers on easel paper. If necessary, use some of these examples to prompt discussion:
- get out of control
- unpredictable
- damaging when it burns things
- hurts people/kills people
- scary/unforgettable
- more powerful than us
- drought/fire restrictions or bans
- playing with matches
- fire: gun powder
- arson

When you have a good set of answers about ways in which fire can be bad, continue:

Ask:
- In what ways can fire be *good*?

Allow time for brainstorming, recording answers on easel paper. If necessary, use some of these examples to prompt discussion:
- light
- warmth
- life giving/sterilize water
- cook
- control environment
- blown glass
- refines metal
- bends metal
- fire clay to make pottery
- candlelight dinner: mood-setter
- exciting, like fireworks

Discuss:

- It seems that fire can be both good and bad. It depends.
- Why do you think God created fire? *(Answers might include: to keep us warm, to help us cook food, to clear land, to create fire breaks.)*
- How do we know that we are using the gift of fire the right way? *(Answers might include: We are old enough to be safe. We know what we are doing. We are protected from the danger. We have reduced the risk. We take time to learn to use it correctly.)*
- How does the way we use fire change as we mature? How are rules about fire different for a two-year-old and a teen?
- *Fire is a good analogy for our sexuality and for sex.* Sexuality is a *gift* from God. It is a gift born of *love* and to be used with love, never as manipulation, in violence, or casually. Using your sexuality when you are not old enough, is full of *risk* and can be *dangerous.*
- *Why* do you think God created sexuality? *(Answers might include: to be close to each other, to make children, to love each other, etc.)*
- How do we know we are using the gift of sexuality in the right way? *(Answers might include: safer sex, be married, be old enough, know the risks.)*
- Using our sexuality wisely is another way of being a good steward.
- Like fire, we can use sexuality in a positive way.
- Sex, like fire, is risky and can be dangerous.
- What could we do to reduce that risk and danger?
- Think about what being a good steward of sexuality means to you.
- We are going to discuss the prompts found in your *Participant Book* on pages 57–58. Write the answers to these prompts in your books as we go along.

Wait until participants have found the proper page in their books, then continue:

- When you think about sexuality and sex, there are many things to consider and remember about being a good steward and staying safe.
- I am going to talk about four things to consider: being *physically safe*, being *knowledgeable*, being *emotionally safe* and being *spiritually ready*:
  - *Being physically safe* means you prepare yourself. It means being in a safe place with a safe person. It means being honest about yourself and why you are thinking of being sexually active. Having sex when you are not ready is not keeping yourself physically safe.
  - *Being knowledgeable* means learning about relationships and your own body. It means considering the risks of your actions and the risks with sexually activity. It means keeping a clear head—and you can't have a clear head while consuming alcohol or drugs; drugs and alcohol inhibit good judgment . . . as does sleep deprivation.
  - *Being emotionally safe* means considering questions such as: Are you being pressured? Are you more concerned about what other people are thinking of you rather than what you think of you? Is your relationship emotionally healthy? Can you talk to and trust the person you are dating?
  - *Being spiritually ready* means understanding that sexuality and love are divine gifts. Ask yourself if you are using these gifts to Glorify God. Is God smiling at you and celebrating?

Once participants have written their answers in their *Participant Books*, continue:
- Let's go back to those words you wrote around the room. Think about our discussion today. Based on our discussion, what other words would you add?
- What words are missing?
- What additional words or thoughts do you want to add?

Divide participants into five groups by having them number off, 1 to 5. Assign each group a different sheet of paper posted on the wall. Ask these five groups to gather at their assigned papers. Say:
- Look at your easel paper and decide what are the most important parts to remember in regard to sexuality and sex.
- Talk about what your group thinks is important.
- I will give you 2 minutes to talk to the people in your group.
- After 2 minutes, I will ask each group to summarize the most important points for the whole group to hear.

After 2 minutes, ask each group to explain what they believe is most important to remember about the topic on the easel paper. This will be a good review for all.

After each group has reported, say:
- Thank you for your summaries.
- Now everyone come back to the large group for our GUIDE and our GO.

Once groups have come back to the larger group say:
- One last thought: "By understanding the full range of sexuality and love with a sense of values you are capable of making responsible and meaningful decisions and to act according to those values."[42]

---

42 *Sexuality: A Divine Gift*, 4.

GUIDE

⏰ 15 minutes

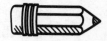

The Facilitator leads this portion of the session.

Pass out small pieces of paper to each participant. Explain:
- Each of you will be writing a question for the Question Box, as you will be asked to do in every session. This is a great place to have your questions answered.
- Everyone needs to write a question. For example, you might ask about a word that you've heard but don't understand or a joke that you don't get. If you don't have a question of your own, think of a question that might be asked by someone your age.
- The Small-Group Leaders and the Facilitator will answer your questions at the beginning of the next session.

The Facilitator moves around the room with the Question Box to collect the questions.

After everyone has submitted a question, invite all participants (leaders and participants) to join in a large enough space where you can form a circle. After you have made the circle, invite everyone to move close enough to each other that they are touching shoulder to shoulder. Invite everyone to relax and take a deep breath. As they relax, they should naturally stop touching shoulders so closely, yet maintain an appropriate level of intimacy for this portion of the session.

Invite all in the circle to close their eyes for a few seconds and slow their breathing. Maintain this for about 30 seconds.

Say:
- When we think about the gift of sexuality, we have lots of hopes and dreams.
- Think about some hopes and dreams you have for one of your friends.

Invite participants to turn to the activity Hopes and Dreams, found on page 58 of the *Participant Book*. Say:

- Complete this letter thinking of your friend.

For your reference, here is the *Friend Hope Letter:*

> Dear Friend, I hope that you know
>> that gifts are . . .
>> that love is . . .
>> that risk-taking means . . .
>> that being safe means . . .
>> and that you are responsible when . . .
>
> Your friend,

Now distribute a blank sheet of paper to each participant. Ask each participant to copy the content of their letter from their *Participant Books* onto this paper.

When participants have finished, collect these letters and post them around the room as a reminder of today's session. When parents pick up their middle-schoolers, show them the letters and explain how the letters summarize today's learning.

GO

⏰ 5 minutes

The Facilitator leads this portion of the session.

Sending participants and leaders back into their daily lives is the final step in the session. This section is meant to be simple and quick.

Say:
- Leaving this time together requires a shift. This is a safe place. This is a place where we are learning and growing together. Outside of this place are our homes, schools, families, friends, and many other social circles.
- What I want to leave you with at the end of each session is that no matter where you are in the world, no matter who you are with, God is with you on your journey.
- Let us close with prayer:

   Leader: The Lord be with you.
   Participants: And also with you.
   Leader: Let us pray.

   May you celebrate today
       with those who love you and those you love.
   May you dance today
       with those closest to you and those far away.
   May you trust you are a child of God
       in your heart and in your soul.
   May you accept forgiveness
       for what you have done and for what you have not done.
   May you claim the beauty all around you
       and pass on the love that surrounds you.
   Amen.

Remember to extinguish the candles and put them (with the matches) in a safe place.

AFTER-THE-SESSION
DEBRIEF

For Facilitator and Small-Group Leaders Only

Please see the full material found in Session 1, page 57.

15–30 minutes

NOTES

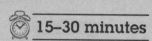

YOU ARE KNOWLEDGEABLE

Knowledge is powerful and empowering.

For wisdom will come into your heart,
and knowledge will be pleasant to your soul;
prudence will watch over you;
and understanding will guard you.
—Proverbs 2:10–11, *NRSV*

OBJECTIVES

❑ Participants will be able to begin determining appropriate personal boundaries for relationships.

❑ Participants will be able to distinguish between facts and fiction about sex and relationships.

❑ Participants will be able to think critically about their own relationships, empowering them to make safe choices.

❑ Participants practice asking questions and grappling with life situations to learn critical thinking skills.

SUPPLIES

❑ pencils or pens (1 per participant)

❑ *These Are Our Bodies Participant Books* (1 per participant)

❑ *These Are Our Bodies Leader Guides* (1 for the Facilitator and 1 for each Small-Group Leader)

NOTES

- ❏ HOPE poster[43] (See pp. 13–14.)
- ❏ easel paper and markers
- ❏ scrap pieces of colored paper for the Question Box (3" x 5")
- ❏ Question Box (See directions, pp. 14–17.)
- ❏ nametags
- ❏ copies of the FACT or FICTION Answer Key, 1 per leader (Appendix, pp. 220–222.)
- ❏ blue painter's tape

....

43 The authors have done their best, without success, to track down the original source of the HOPE acronym. No copyright infringement is intended. If notified, they will gladly credit the original author in future editions of *These Are Our Bodies*.

PREPARATION

- ❏ GATHER needed supplies.
- ❏ Set up the room for the session. Arrange furniture and materials so that they are readily available and designed for discussion.
- ❏ Have the FACT or FICTION signs ready to be put on the floor during today's GAME. (See directions on p. 148.)

GATHER

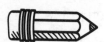

 20 minutes

As participants enter, have them put on their nametags, pick up their *Participant Books,* and select a pencil or pen.

HOPE Poster

Gain participants' attention and say:
- Welcome everyone. As we begin today, *(name of participant)* is going to lead us in today's GATHER.
- Who would like to lead us next week?

Make a note of the volunteer for next week.

Participant says:
- Let's look together at our HOPE poster.
- Stand and join me as we read together:

Honesty: We commit to sharing what we really think.
Openness: We commit to being open to what others say, both our group members and our leaders, and most of all to God.
Privacy: We commit to keeping what is said and done here within this space.
Enthusiasm: We commit to laughter, fun, and a sense of wonder.

Prayer

Lead participants in this prayer:

Holy God, one who took on flesh and lived as one of us,
dwell with us here and give us courage to learn, grow,
    and become more like you—
loving, kind, and full of grace—
through God our Creator, Christ our Redeemer,
and the Spirit our Sustainer. *Amen.*

Say:
- Thank you *(name of participant)* for leading us in our GATHER.

The Question Box

Note: Be sure you have read the full explanation of the Question Box found on pages 14–17 of the Introduction. Please see the full material found in Session 3, page 83.

The Facilitator reads one question and says:
- *(Small-Group Leader's name)* is going to answer that question.

Repeat until all the questions have been answered.

Guidelines for answering questions:

- Think about the time that it will take to answer the questions. An average of 60–90 seconds per question is a reasonable guideline. Answering questions for a group of 6–8 participants will take 8–12 minutes.
- Adjust the amount of time that you allow based on your group.
- Do not over-explain. Keep it moving!
- Go down the question list one by one and answer each question. The Small-Group Leaders and the Facilitator will have already decided how to answer each question and who will answer the question at the end of last session.
- Remember to answer the questions clearly and concisely. You are aiming for a 45–60 second answer.
- Don't belabor the answers. You will want to spend as much time on the session as you can.

When all the questions have been answered, say:
- You all asked great questions.
- Remember that you will have an opportunity to write a question for the Question Box at the end of this session.

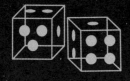

GAME

NOTES

FACT or FICTION

 20 minutes

For each session's Game, consider moving the group to an alternative location—another area of the same room, another room, a space outdoors, etc. Young people benefit from movement and a change of seating.

For today's game, we define a FACT as a statement that can be proven by science, medicine, and modern research. We use the word FICTION to mean a popular misconception or rumor.

In other settings, a game like this might be called *Truth or Myth*. As leaders, avoid using the words *truth* and *myth* since, within our faith tradition, both have significant meaning. *Myth* can refer to deep meaning found in sacred texts and cultures, embedded collection of stories that, though factually not necessarily true, carry real meaning and truth. The word and concept of *truth* is also meaningful and often refers to the deeper truths in the realm of our spiritual lives that are beyond fact.

You may want to change location. For this game a large open space with just chairs is best. Divide the room with blue painters tape into two sides. Label one side of the room with big letters made out of the tape spelling the word *FACT*. Use tape to label the other side *FICTION*.

In this game, statements are meant to primarily address what was taught in Session 2 as "biological sex." Many of the statements have to do with sexual intercourse and human anatomy. Whenever possible, use terminology from Session 1 in the activity.

Say:

- In this game, when we call out "FACT or FICTION?" you will decide whether a statement we have read is FACT or FICTION by standing on one side of the room or the other.

- You can see the line here in the middle and the categories on either side. This side is FACT *(point)* and this side is FICTION *(point)*.
- For this game, a FACT is a statement that can be proven by science, medicine, and modern research, and FICTION is a popular misconception or rumor.

Read each statement aloud, then call out "FACT or FICTION?" Give participants to the count of 5 to pick FACT or FICTION by walking to one side of the room or the other.

Keep the FACT or FICTION Answer Key close to you. After participants move, take a moment and tell them the answer and explain the answer if needed. You could ask Small-Group Leaders to play and to choose the wrong answers as well!

Note: Participants will find the FACT or FICTION statements, along with commentary, in their *Participant Books* on pages 62–69. There is also space for "debriefing" after the game on pages 70–72.

GRAPPLE

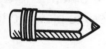

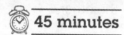 **45 minutes**

Small-Group Leaders should turn to this page (150) in the *Leader Guide* to follow along.

Today's GRAPPLE begins with discussion between pairs of participants, then moves into large-group sharing.

Info for Facilitators and Small-Group Leaders:
- Expect some participants to feel frustrated because they won't have all the information that they need to make a sound decision.
- Guide participants to ask questions that would help them in a similar situation.
- One of the objectives is to give participants an opportunity to wrestle with things that are not clear and to recognize that the assumptions we make can be unhelpful.
- Both in the game and the discussion to follow, avoid looking for one correct answer. Instead, guide participants toward understanding that the benefit comes from thinking and analyzing these situations before they face similar situations. For example, in Situation #5, participants may discover that there are perspectives and facts that they do not know. Perhaps they would like to hear why Jane thinks it *isn't* a good idea to walk to the mall. Why might it *not* be okay to walk to the mall? Some questions they might ask are: "Is it a safety issue? Is it a matter of not telling her parents her plans?" We want participants to struggle with the vagueness of this situation to practice asking discerning questions.
- The ability to think critically and apply their faith and values is a lifelong skill worthy of teaching.

Say to participants:
- In a moment we are going to play another game called The Situation Game. It is meant to help you think through how you would respond—and what advice you might give—to someone in a certain situation.

Divide the group into pairs by having participants line up in order of their birthdays. Once they are lined up, have the first two people be partners, then the second two. Continue creating the pairs until everyone has been paired. If you have an odd number of participants, make one group of three.

Invite participants to turn to pages 73–76 in their *Participant Books*, where they will find the situations for the game. You may want to assign certain situations to certain pairs or ask each pair to pick its own.

Say:
- Take turns reading a situation. Discuss with your partner how you could answer the two questions that follow that situation.
- Write the answers to those questions in your *Participant Book* in the space provided.
- When the time is up for discussing in pairs, we will come back together to share.
- With your partner, together find a place where you can complete the exercise without being disturbed or disturbing others.

Let pairs get started. Walk around the room, taking time to sit with each pair for a few minutes. Encourage the Small-Group Leaders to guide pairs. Spending a few moments with a pair should not inhibit its discussion.

At the end of about 15–20 minutes, invite participants back together to report on what they discussed with their partners:
- Let's start with the first situation. When you read the first situation, what did you think the parents should do?
- What factors did your group think of that the teen and the parents should consider?
- Did you have anything else that you discussed related to the first situation?

Continue:
- Let's talk about Situation #2. What advice did you think to give the teen?
- What factors did your group think of that the teen should consider?
- Did you have anything else that you discussed related to Situation #2?

Continue on in this same pattern as you work through all six situations. When done, discuss:
- What have we learned from talking about these situations?
- What are some questions that we can ask ourselves when we find ourselves in difficult situations?

The Facilitator can write the questions on easel paper to capture participants' thoughts and feelings.

Continue:
- As you grow and learn, you will gain new freedoms and privileges. You will become more independent. With new freedoms and privileges comes more responsibility. Sometimes what you want and what your parents want may seem like opposites. Remember:
  - Parents are thinking about your safety.
  - You think about independence.

- º Parents like a plan.
- º You like to be spontaneous.
- º Parents often see the unexpected consequences.
- º You don't always have the experience to see the consequences clearly.
- º Parents want you to grow into your independence.
- º You are sometimes in a hurry to grow up.
- º Parents want middle-schoolers to be successful with new freedoms and situations.
- º You want to have *fun!*
- There are a few things that will help you as you navigate new situations and new freedoms:
  - º Make a clear plan with your friends and your parents.
  - º Stick with the plan—don't make last-minute changes to the plan.
  - º Talk about the new situation with your parents and brainstorm things that you may need to know.
  - º If you get to an event or someone's house and what you thought was the plan is not the plan, call your parents for a ride home. You don't have to stay in a situation in which you feel uncomfortable.

GUIDE

NOTES

The Facilitator leads this portion of the session.

Pass out small pieces of paper to each participant. Explain:
- Each of you will be writing a question for the Question Box, as you will be asked to do in every session. This is a great place to have your questions answered.
- Everyone needs to write a question. For example, you might ask about a word that you've heard but don't understand or a joke that you don't get. If you don't have a question of your own, think of a question that might be asked by someone your age.
- The Small-Group Leaders and the Facilitator will answer your questions at the beginning of the next session.

The Facilitator moves around the room with the Question Box to collect the questions.

After everyone has submitted a question, say:
- Let's all gather together in a circle. That includes participants *and* Small-Group Leaders. Participants, bring your *Participant Books* with you.

Once gathered, say:
- There are many ideas out there about sex. Some of them are fact; some are fiction. Sometimes, the same thing can be true about our faith. Some would say that God and sex, or faith and sex are very separate topics. One of the main goals of these sessions is to prove that is FICTION.
- As we close this session, I want us to bring the topic back toward where God is in the midst of these situations. Situations like the ones you worked on in small groups happen every day in your lives.
- What is really cool about the Bible, the book that Christians hold up and use as a GUIDE for life, is that it is filled with similar situations. The authors and people in the stories of the Bible may not have had our technology, but they had our drama!

- For our GUIDE time, you need to turn to pages 78–79 in your *Participant Books*. On these pages there are verses to choose from. They are verses that uplift and remind us that, even in tricky situations, God is always with us.

Make sure participants have found the right page. Give them 2–3 minutes of silence to read through the choices.

Continue:
- When you are ready, read out loud the verse that struck you the most.
- More than one person may read the same verse.
- The words are always good, always filled with love and grace.

Take time to let participants and Small-Group Leaders speak their verses out loud. After everyone has had a turn, close with:
- All of these words we hear as followers of God the Father, Jesus the Son, and the Holy Spirit our guide. *Amen*.

GO

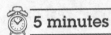
NOTES

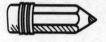

The Facilitator leads this portion of the session.

Sending participants and leaders back into their daily lives is the final step in the session. This section is meant to be simple and quick.

Say:

- Leaving this time together requires a shift. This is a safe place. This is a place where we are learning and growing together. Outside of this place are our homes, schools, families, friends, and many other social circles.
- What I want to leave you with at the end of each session is that no matter where you are in the world, no matter who you are with, God is with you on your journey.
- Let us close with prayer:

  Leader: The Lord be with you.
  Participants: And also with you.
  Leader: Let us pray.

God, the King eternal, whose light divides the day from the night and turns the shadow of death into the morning: Drive far from us all wrong desires, incline our hearts to keep your law, and guide our feet into the way of peace; that, having done your will with cheerfulness during the day, we may, when night comes, rejoice to give you thanks; through Jesus Christ our Lord. *Amen.*[44]

44 Book of Common Prayer, A Collect for the Renewal of Life, page 99.

AFTER · THE · SESSION
DEBRIEF

For Facilitator and Small-Group Leaders Only

Please see the full material found in Session 1, page 57.

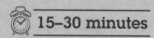
15–30 minutes

NOTES

SESSION 8
YOU ARE CONNECTED

In a sense, religious education begins before we are even
aware of such distinctions as body, soul, and mind.
The life of the body, the life of the mind, and the life of
the soul are all inextricably interwoven. Our children
are temples of the Spirit of God—the Spirit who binds
together body, soul and mind.[45]

— J. Bradley Wigger

....

45 Wigger, J. Bradley, *The Power of God at Home: Nurturing Our Children in Love and Grace*, (San
   Francisco: Jossey-Bass, 2003), 159.

OBJECTIVES

- ❑ Parents and middle-schoolers experience value clarification exercises together.
- ❑ Parents and middle-schoolers learn about the importance listening plays in relationships.
- ❑ Parents and middle-schoolers practice listening to one another during the Parent and Teen interviews.

SUPPLIES

- ❑ pencils or pens (1 per participant and parent)
- ❑ *These Are Our Bodies Participant Book* (1 per participant)
- ❑ *These Are Our Bodies Participant Book Leader Guide* (1 for the Facilitator and 1 for each Small-Group Leader)
- ❑ *These Are Our Bodies Parent Books* (1 per parent)

NOTES

_____
_____
_____
_____
_____
_____
_____
_____
_____
_____
_____
_____
_____
_____
_____
_____
_____
_____
_____

- ❑ HOPE[46] poster (See pp. 13–14)
- ❑ easel paper and markers
- ❑ nametags
- ❑ 5 sheets of 8½" x 11" paper with one word or phrase on each piece of paper: *strongly agree, agree, no opinion, disagree*, and *strongly disagree* (These are the five signs to be used in today's GAME, 5 to Decide.)

....

46 The authors have done their best, without success, to track down the original source of the HOPE acronym. No copyright infringement is intended. If notified, they will gladly credit the original author in future editions of *These Are Our Bodies*.

PREPARATION

- ❑ Gather needed supplies.
- ❑ Set up the room for the session. Arrange furniture and materials so that they are readily available and designed for discussion.
- ❑ Tape the Signs for 5 to Decide on the wall along the room or place on the floor linearly.

GATHER

NOTES

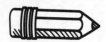

 20 minutes

As participants enter, have them put on their nametags, pick up their *Participant Books*, and select a pencil or pen.

HOPE Poster

Gain participants' attention and say:

- Welcome everyone. As we begin today, *(name of participant)* is going to lead us in today's GATHER.
- Who would like to lead us next week?

Make a note of the volunteer for next week.

Participant says:

- Let's look together at our HOPE poster.
- Stand and join me as we read together:

Honesty: We commit to sharing what we really think.
Openness: We commit to being open to what others say, both our group members and our leaders, and most of all to God.
Privacy: We commit to keeping what is said and done here within this space.
Enthusiasm: We commit to laughter, fun, and a sense of wonder.

Prayer

Lead participants in this prayer:

> Holy God, one who took on flesh and lived as one of us,
> dwell with us here and give us courage to learn, grow,
>   and become more like you—
> loving, kind, and full of grace—
> through God our Creator, Christ our Redeemer,
> and the Spirit our Sustainer. *Amen*.

Note: Since this is a session with the parents, you will not be using the Question Box.

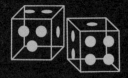

GAME

Five to Decide

 20 minutes

Put the sheets of paper on which you have written *strongly agree, agree, no opinion, disagree,* and *strongly disagree* on the floor *or* post them on the wall.

Say:

- I am going to read a series of statements.
- When a statement is read, go stand beside the sheet of paper that represents your response to the statement.
- If you are a participant, you may choose *not* to respond to a statement.
- Parents, we would like *you* to respond to every statement. Be brave!
- Just like in many of our games, you have a limited amount of time to make a decision. When I read the statement I will countdown from *5* and you have to "decide" by the time I reach *1*. Thus the name . . . *Five to Decide!*
- Part of the fun in deciding quickly what you think about the statement is quickly moving to the *strongly agree, agree, no opinion, disagree,* or *strongly disagree* part of the room. Are you ready?

Read a statement, then counting down: *5, 4, 3, 2, 1.* Repeat for all the statements.

After each "time of decision," pause to ask a few parents and participants to discuss why they chose their particular position. Do be very careful *not* to be judgmental about people's choices.

Feel free to add some of your own statements to the list.

Be mindful to read the statements so that people are moving around the room as they agree and disagree with the statements. Some of the statements most people will agree with, so try to intersperse those statements with statements that bring more varied responses.

Statements:

- Pizza is the perfect lunch.
- The church is a resource for me in difficult times in my life.
- Whistling at good-looking people is fine.
- Males and females should share equally in housework, childcare, and yard work.
- Throwing eggs at cars is a harmless prank.
- Bullying online is better than teasing someone in person.
- Toilet papering someone's yard is completely okay.
- It is better to go to the beach than mountains for vacation.
- I felt a little weird about being here at this event.
- It can be difficult to stand up for how I feel, especially when it would mean going against my friends.
- Gossiping is hurtful, and Christians should not gossip.
- It is okay to cheat if everyone in the class is cheating.
- Marriage is a lifetime commitment.
- I feel comfortable talking about sexuality.
- Love is the only important consideration in choosing whom to marry.
- If two high-school participants are in love and are planning to get married after high school, it is okay for them to have sex.
- God doesn't have much to do with dating.
- The church is a resource for me in the good times of my life.
- Looks and chemistry are the main ingredients in two people being sexually attractive to each other.

Return to large group. Invite participants and parents to reflect on the GAME. Invite conversation, and be accepting of differing opinions.

Discuss:

- What did you learn about your child?
- What did you learn about your parents?
- What questions surprised you the most?
- Which responses surprised you the most?

GRAPPLE

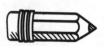

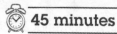 **45 minutes**

For today's GRAPPLE, parents will need their *Parent Books* and participants will need their *Participant Books.*

Info for Facilitators and Small-Group Leaders:
- Parents and their middle-schoolers are navigating rough waters when they practice vulnerability with each other. Your role is that of supporter and cheerleader. If you see someone in need of encouragement, offer a kind word or pat on the shoulder to affirm them.
- Be sure to offer plenty of space for parents and participants to spread out and find a quiet nook when they interview each other. Vulnerability is inhibited by the possibility of overheard conversations.

Explain:
- At this time we are going to break into parent and participant small groups. You will find an *Interview Guide* for this activity in your *Participant Book* on pages 82–84 and in your *Parent Book* on pages 62–63.
- In a moment I will ask you to begin the interviews with each teen interviewing his or her parents first. After 5–6 minutes, I will ask you to switch and have the parents interview the participants. After another 5–6 minutes, I will call everyone back to the larger group.
- Remember to respect the privacy of others and to keep your voices low enough that you do not disrupt the interview of another family. In the event that the time is up but you have not yet finished, you can finish the interview at home.

Note: For your reference, you will find the interview questions printed on page 223 in the Appendix.

After 5–6 minutes, ask the families to switch and have the parents interview the participants.

Ask:

- How did the interviews go?
- Middle-schoolers, what did you learn about your parents?

Say:

- I am sure each family had a unique experience in the interviews.
- It is the hope of this session for you to see that you are connected . . . we are in this together, participants, parents, and the church.
- We should always work to have good communication with one another in our families.

GUIDE

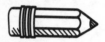

NOTES

 15 minutes

Invite all participants (leaders and participants) to join you in a large enough space where everyone can form a circle.

Say:

- As we prepare to bring this session to a close, I want to invite each person here to reflect on the experience of interviewing another person. In some ways, I wonder if the interviews you conducted could be compared to a story in the Old Testament.
- It is a story of a conversation with God. This story reminds us that a conversation is supposed to include listening. Sometimes we can forget how important it is to listen to each other. The story is also a good metaphor for the conversations that you had with each other.
- In the story of Elijah in 1 Kings 19, Elijah has a conversation with God. The Bible tells us that Elijah had spent the night in a cave—Elijah was feeling very far away from God. The conversation he had with God is beautiful and surprising.
- The word of the Lord told Elijah to go outside of the cave and wait for the Lᴏʀᴅ to pass by (1 Kings 19:11). At first, there was a great wind that split the mountains and broke rocks into pieces (1 Kings 19:11). Then there was an earthquake and then a fire (1 Kings 19:12). In the story we are told that the Lᴏʀᴅ was not in the wind, the fire, or the earthquake. Finally, the passage says, "And after the fire a sound of sheer silence," (1 Kings 19:12 *NRSV*).
- It was in the silence that Elijah came out of the cave and spoke with God. Silence[47] is a gentle, beautiful, and sometimes surprising thing. Often as family and friends, we can show our love for each other without any words. We can give a hug, listen with empathy, or squeeze a hand.

....

47 You might have someone who thinks about silence in a negative way. Sometimes people might see silence as retaliation or a weapon. That really isn't the type of silence that we are introducing here. In this situation, we are really talking about the gift of silence that we give one another. The gift that says, "I love you enough to listen. To quiet the voice in my head, to hear and accept you—just as you are." You might want to remind the group that this lesson is about *connection*, about connecting to God and to each other. Our hope is that they will practice being more connected.

- Today you practiced listening and sharing. You were able to truly be heard and to hear someone else. That is a gift that you gave each other.
- Our hope is that your family will have many more times with each other—to listen and to speak. To hear and to be heard.
- If you were going to describe your interview today, would you call it a great wind? an earthquake? a fire?
- I invite you to describe your interview as one of these three images: *wind, fire,* or *earthquake*. For example, you might say, "My interview was like a *fire* because it _____."

When all of the parents and participants have spoken, continue with the GO portion of the session.

 **GO**

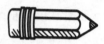

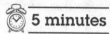 **5 minutes**

Sending participants, parents, and leaders back into their daily lives is the final step in the session. This section is meant to be simple and quick.

Say:
- Just as Elijah found God in the form of silence, so let us take a moment to collect our thoughts in silence. In this time of silence, may our focus shift from all that we heard and all that we said to all that God wants for us.
- Breathe in deeply the silence that can fill up your heart with the love of God.

Let the group maintain silence for about one minute.

Say:
- Leaving this time together requires a shift. This is a safe place. This is a place where we are learning and growing together. Outside of this place are our homes, schools, families, friends, and many other social circles.
- Remember, no matter where you are in the world, no matter who you are with, God is with you on your journey.

Let us close with prayer.

Leader: The Lord be with you.
Participants and Parents: And also with you.
Leader: Let us pray.

Teach me to listen, O God, to those nearest me, my family, my friends, my neighbors.
Help me to be aware that no matter what words I hear,
the message is, "Accept the person I am. Listen to me."
Teach me to listen, my caring God, to those far from me—the whisper of the hopeless, the plea of the forgotten, the cry of the anguished.

Teach me to listen, O God my Mother, to myself. Help me to be less afraid to trust the voice inside in the deepest part of me.

Teach me to listen, Holy Spirit, for your voice—in busyness and in boredom, in certainty and doubt, in noise and in silence.

Teach me, Lord, to listen.

Amen.[48]

48 John Veltri, S.J. in Harter, Michael *Hearts on Fire: Praying with Jesuits* (Chicago: Loyola Press, 2004), 30.

AFTER·THE·SESSION
DEBRIEF

For Facilitator and Small-Group Leaders Only

Please see the full material found in Session 1, page 57.

15–30 minutes

NOTES

YOU ARE EMPOWERED

Therefore, if there is any encouragement in Christ, any comfort in love, any sharing in the Spirit, any sympathy, complete my joy by thinking the same way, having the same love, being united, and agreeing with each other. Don't do anything for selfish purposes, but with humility think of others as better than yourselves. Instead of each person watching out for their own good, watch out for what is better for others. Adopt the attitude that was in Christ Jesus.

—Philippians 2:2–5, *CEB*

Christians, who have developed an understanding of the full range and types of love and have a clear sense of values and decision-making skills, will not fear their sexual nature. They have the capacity to make responsible, meaningful decisions and to act accordingly.[49]

OBJECTIVE

- ❑ Participants will become empowered through knowledge about the topics of refusal skills, sex for sale, aggressiveness and assertiveness, sexually transmitted infections, tech safety, and birth control.
- ❑ Build confidence with the language around important topics
- ❑ Enjoy learning in non-intimidating way

....

49 Sex Education for Mission & Ministry Unit. *Sexuality: A Divine Gift* (New York: Domestic and Foreign Missionary Society, 1987), 4.

SUPPLIES

- ❑ pencils or pens (1 per participant)
- ❑ *These Are Our Bodies Participant Book* (1 per participant)
- ❑ *These Are Our Bodies Leader Guide* (1 for the Facilitator and 1 for each Small-Group Leader)
- ❑ HOPE poster[50] (See pp. 13–14.)
- ❑ easel paper and markers
- ❑ scrap pieces of colored paper for the Question Box (3" x 5")
- ❑ Question Box (See directions, pp. 14–17.)
- ❑ nametags
- ❑ 2 copies of the Game Board for Can You Name This? (Appendix, p. 228.)
- ❑ 2 sets of Can You Name This? Word Cards (Appendix, p. 229)
- ❑ game board for Jeopardy

....

50 The authors have done their best, without success, to track down the original source of the HOPE acronym. No copyright infringement is intended. If notified, they will gladly credit the original author in future editions of *These Are Our Bodies.*

NOTES

Note: You can download the game board (in PowerPoint) for Jeopardy from https://www .churchpublishing.org/theseareourbodiesmsleader or create your own board. To create your own Jeopardy game board you will need a sheet of 3" x 5" poster board, a yard stick to draw lines, markers, and square Post-it Notes.® Draw a grid on the poster board of six rows and six columns. The first horizontal row contains the names of the categories. The second horizontal row will have Post-it Notes with $100, the third horizontal row will have post-it notes with $200, the fourth horizontal row will have $300, the fifth horizontal row will have $400, and the sixth horizontal row will be $500. Use Post-it Notes in each square to write the names of the categories and dollar amounts, as illustrated below. Once you make the board, you can use it to play other Jeopardy games by changing the categories (simply with new Post-it Notes). In the homemade version, the answers are not on the board. You use the board to keep track of which categories and dollar amounts have been chosen. See an example online at https://www.churchpublishing.org/ theseareourbodiesmsleader. When playing, participants choose the category and dollar amount, either advance the electronic game or manually remove the sticky note to show that it has been chosen.

Handmade Jeopardy Game Board

Refusal Skills	Sex for Sale	Aggressive vs Assertive	STIs	Tech Talk	Birth Control
$100	$100	$100	$100	$100	$100
$200	$200	$200	$200	$200	$200
$300	$300	$300	$300	$300	$300
$400	$400	$400	$400	$400	$400
$500	$500	$500	$500	$500	$500

Downloadable Jeopardy Game Board

PREPARATION

- ❏ Gather needed supplies.
- ❏ The Facilitator will divide the groups before the session starts and assign two Small-Group Leaders to each group. Each group should have 4–6 participants of different genders and different schools. The Facilitator will want to think about the formation of the groups to ensure that cliques are not formed. Use the nametags to delineate the groups. One group could have blue borders on the nametags and the other red. Another way is to put a different sticker on the nametags, for example, one group could have star stickers and the other group happy-face stickers. Deciding on the groups before the session saves time and also makes the session go more smoothly. If you have 4–6 participants, do the following activity as one group. You can use these same groups for the GRAPPLE section as well.
- ❏ Set up the room for the session. Arrange furniture and materials so that they are readily available and designed for discussion.
- ❏ Set up computer and projector to project the Jeopardy Board (if using the online version) or have the Jeopardy poster ready to play (if using a homemade version).

GATHER

 5 minutes

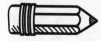

As participants enter, have them put on their nametags, pick up their *Participant Books*, and select a pencil or pen.

HOPE Poster

Gain participants' attention and say:
- Welcome everyone. As we begin today, *(name of participant)* is going to lead us in today's GATHER.
- Who would like to lead us next week?

Make a note of the volunteer for next week.

Participant says:
- Let's look together at our HOPE poster.
- Stand and join me as we read together.

  Honesty: We commit to sharing what we really think.
  Openness: We commit to being open to what others say, both our group members and our leaders, and most of all to God.
  Privacy: We commit to keeping what is said and done here within this space.
  Enthusiasm: We commit to laughter, fun, and a sense of wonder.

Prayer

Lead participants in this prayer:

  Holy God, one who took on flesh and lived as one of us,
  dwell with us here and give us courage to learn, grow,
      and become more like you,
  that we may be more loving, kind, and full of grace,
  through God our Creator, Christ our Redeemer, and the Spirit our
  Sustainer. *Amen.*

The Question Box

Note: Be sure you have read the full explanation of the Question Box found on pages 14–17 of the Introduction. Please see the full material found in Session 3, page 83.

Guidelines for answering questions:

- ➤ Think about the time that it will take to answer the questions. An average of 60–90 seconds per question is a reasonable guideline. Answering questions for a group of 6–8 participants will take 8–12 minutes.
- ➤ Adjust the amount of time that you allow based on your group.
- ➤ Do not over-explain. Keep it moving!
- ➤ Go down the question list one by one and answer each question. The Small-Group Leaders and the Facilitator will have already decided how to answer each question and who will answer the question at the end of last session.
- ➤ Remember to answer the questions clearly and concisely. You are aiming for a 45–60 second answer.
- ➤ Don't belabor the answers. You will want to spend as much time on the session as you can.

When all the questions have been answered, say:
- You all asked great questions.
- Remember that you will have an opportunity to write a question for the Question Box at the end of this session.

GAME

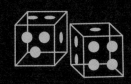

Can You Name This?

 20 minutes

Can You Name This? is a matching game designed to review basic anatomy. This vocabulary should not be new to middle-schoolers, although they may still need help and encouragement while playing; the objective of the game is to remind participants of the terms, not to embarrass them. Small-Group Leaders can give as much help as participants need to feel successful and comfortable about playing the game. Remember that some participants may need encouragement and support using the words for genitalia. Give participants hints if they need more help. Independence and mastery of the terms are not the goal—exposure to the words and hearing them used is the main goal of the game.

Before playing, print and cut apart the Word Cards found on page 229 in the Appendix. Here, for your reference, is the list of words found on the cards:

- uterus
- cervix
- vulva
- testicle or testes
- urethra
- bladder
- sperm duct
- prostate gland
- vagina
- penis
- fallopian tube
- vas deferens
- ovary
- scrotum

Remind participants that questions about the topics covered in the session can come up even *after* the session through the Question Box.

Begin:
- How many of you have ever played a matching game?
- We are going to play a game called, Can You Name This? You will play as a small group and work together to put anatomical terms (about your bodies) in the correct spot on a diagram.

Hold up one of the Game Boards with the anatomy drawing (found in the Appendix on p. 228) and a set of the Game Cards (Appendix, p. 229). Continue:
- This is the Game Board for Can You Name This? and these are the Word Cards.
- Your team will put your Game Board in the middle of your group circle. You will then put your stack of Word Cards (there are 14 of them) face down on the Game Board.
- Take turns, one at a time, picking a card, reading it, and placing it on the board beside the diagram where that part of the body is found. Remember that this is a team game; the whole team can help decide where the term should go. If you need to move some terms around as the game progresses, that is okay as well.
- You will have 10 minutes to play.
- Move into your teams now and take a Game Board and a set of Word Cards.

Wait for the teams to get into place, then say:
- Are you ready? Set . . . GO!

Begin timing. Hopefully everyone finishes well under the 10-minute mark. It is possible that groups will take less time; that is okay.

When both groups have finished—or time has elapsed—ask participants to stop.

GRAPPLE

 45 minutes

Participants remain in their small groups from the GAME. Invite each Small-Group Leader to turn to this page (179) in the *Leader Guides* to follow along.

Info for Facilitators and Small-Group Leaders:
- Participants are learning a great deal of information in this session. Expect that additional questions will come up in the Question Box. In addition, anticipate the need for follow-up conversations that occur naturally as the session unfolds.
- All of the answers for the questions in Jeopardy are in the Expert Info pages found in the Participant Guide (pp. 86–100). Familiarize yourself with these Expert Info pages so that when you are asked questions you will know what participants have already read.
- After the Facilitator explains the rules for Jeopardy, listed next, post a summary of the rules to help everyone remember how to play.

Summary of the Rules for poster board:
- The most important rules for Jeopardy are:
  - Work as a team.
  - Have Fun.
  - Learn!
- And here is how to play:
  - Each team needs to choose a *spokesperson* and a *time-keeper*.
  - The teams will take turns answering the questions.
  - If a team misses a question, the other team can steal that question (by answering correctly) for half the dollar amount.
  - The question will be read once. After the question is read, the answering team has 30 seconds to answer.
  - The *spokesperson* actually gives the answer, after the teams confers.
  - If a team does *not* confer, no points are given . . . so *always* talk it over with your teammates. Don't just blurt out an answer.

Verbally share these rules with participants:

- The most important rules for Jeopardy are:
  - ○ Work as a team.
  - ○ Have Fun.
  - ○ Learn!
- And here is how to play:
  - ○ First, divide into two teams from the previous game. It is easier if the groups are the same in both the GAME and the GRAPPLE
  - ○ In your team, choose a *spokesperson* and a *time-keeper*.
  - ○ The teams will take turns answering the questions.
  - ○ If a team misses a question, the other team can steal that question (by answering correctly) for half the dollar amount.
  - ○ The question will be read once. After the question is read, the answering team has 30 seconds to answer.
  - ○ The *spokesperson* actually gives the answer, after the teams confers.
  - ○ If a team does *not* confer, no points are given . . . so *always* talk it over with your teammates. Don't just blurt out an answer.

Continue:

- The game of Jeopardy has been around for many years. If you are not familiar with it, that is okay, because I am going to explain it to you.
- In the game, there are six categories of questions. Each category corresponds to the six Expert Info topics found in your *Participant Guide* on pages 86–100. The topics are:
  - ○ refusal skills
  - ○ sex for sale
  - ○ aggressive versus assertive
  - ○ sexually transmitted infections
  - ○ tech talk
  - ○ birth control
- In Jeopardy, each team takes turns answering questions about the 6 topics.
- In the show on TV, the questions and answers are reversed; the game host reads an answer and the contestant responds with the question. In our game you will be asked a question, and you will give the answer.
- All of the information you need for the answers is in your *Participant Books*. You have Expert Info for each topic that you will use to play the game.
- To get started, your team will assign a different person in your group to read each of the Expert Info pages to themself. That way there will be at least one person in your group who has read the information on each topic and can help answer the questions in that category.
- If you have six participants in your group, each participant will read one section of Expert Info for one topic. If you have more than six, two people can read the same Expert Info on a particular topic. If you have fewer than six, ask for a volunteer to read about more than one section of Expert info.

Have Small-Group Leaders make sure participants are actually reading the Expert Info in their *Participant Books*. For your reference, the Expert Info as it appears in the *Participant Book* is printed in the Appendix on pages 230–241.

The Small-Group Leaders say to their groups:
- Everyone turn to page 86 in your *Participant Book*. Let's assign each of you a topic to read. Who wants Refusal Skills? Who wants Sex for Sale? Who wants Assertive vs. Aggressive? Who wants STIs (Sexually Transmitted Infections)? Who wants to read Tech Talk? Who wants Birth Control?
- After you read your assigned Expert Info, you can read the other topics if you'd like and there's time. Remember we are all going to answer the questions *together*.
- You have the advantage of working as a group. You have the disadvantage of only having one person who has read the entire Expert Info on each topic.
- The expert who read the Expert Info does not have the final say for your group answer, but you may want to consider how much knowledge they have compared to the rest of the group.

The Facilitator says:
- For the next 6 minutes, everyone is going to read.

Once the 6 minutes is up, continue:
- Now that you are all experts on at least your topic, we are almost ready to start playing.
- Each team has chosen a *spokesperson* who will give the final answer of the group. The *spokesperson* can read the answer from the Expert Info pages, if you want to. Who will be the *spokesperson* for this team? And for this team?
- Each team has also chosen a *timer-keeper*. Once the question is read, the team answering the question has 30 seconds to decide its answer. The *timekeeper* also calls time for the other team! Who will be the timekeeper for this team? And for this team?
- Each team will take turns finding the answer to the question.

The teams need to confer before answering each question. If the answer is not exact, that is okay. Try to monitor the game, so the dollar amounts are fairly close to each other. Give your team some hints or help if they are behind in dollars. Don't emphasize competition in the game; the objectives are to have fun, gain information, and build the confidence of participants.

Say:
- I will read each question only once, so listen carefully. Once the question has been read, time begins. Remember you have 30 seconds as a whole team to confer (work together). The whole team will decide the answer and the *spokesperson* will tell me the answer.
- When it is your team's turn, the *spokesperson* will choose the category and the dollar amount for the answer, for example the *spokesperson* might say, "STIs for $100."
- Let's decide which team will go first. Let's have the *time-keeper* choose a number between 1 and 10.

Ask one team *spokesperson:*
- What's your number?

Ask the other team *spokesperson:*
- What's your number?

Say:
- Team _____ had the closest number to my number 7. This team will go first.
- *Spokesperson,* choose a category and a dollar amount.

As participants choose the category and dollar amount, either advance the electronic game or manually remove the Post-it Note to show that it has been chosen.

Use the Jeopardy Question Sheet (Appendix, pp. 224–227) to read the questions. Remember (Jeopardy fans), participants do not respond in the form of a question!

As the game progresses, the Facilitator can explain any of the answers that might need additional explanation. Since one of the purposes is to teach basic information, you can emphasize certain information by reiterating or expanding on the topic.

Play the game until half the board has been used or until the energy for the game dwindles. When the game is finished, say:
- Becoming an expert in *all* of these areas is truly important.
- In this session it was not realistic for anyone to memorize or completely understand all that was said.
- After the session, please read over the pages in your *Participant Book* again. Ask more questions through our Question Box. Talk to your parents, your Small-Group Leaders, or to me.

GUIDE

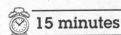 **15 minutes**

The Facilitator leads this portion of the session.

Pass out small pieces of paper to each participant. Explain:
- Each of you will be writing a question for the Question Box, as you will be asked to do in every session. This is a great place to have your questions answered.
- Everyone one needs to write a question. For example, you might ask about a word that you've heard but don't understand or a joke that you don't get. If you don't have a question of your own, think of a question that might be asked by someone your age.
- The Small-Group Leaders and the Facilitator will answer your questions at the beginning of the next session.

The Facilitator moves around the room with the Question Box to collect the questions.

After everyone has submitted a question, invite all participants (leaders and participants) to join in a large enough space where you can form a circle. After you have made the circle, invite everyone to move close enough to each other that they are touching shoulder to shoulder. Invite everyone to relax and take a deep breath. As they relax, they should naturally stop touching shoulders so closely, yet maintain an appropriate level of intimacy for this portion of the session.

Invite all in the circle to close their eyes for a few seconds and slow their breathing. Maintain this for about 30 seconds.

Say:
- We know it is impossible for you to truly be an expert on all that you just read today, so we encourage you to go back over each section of Expert Info with your parents and by yourself. Bring your questions back to the Question Box or ask your parents.
- The title of this session included the word *EMPOWERED*. At the root of this word is the word *POWER*. As we reflect on what we did in this session, remember that *knowledge is power.* No one

can take away from you the things you have learned here today. You have the power to make wise and educated choices because you are able to become an expert.

- Though we normally use this time to encourage one another, this session had a greater emphasis on what each person will take away. So for this time together, let's take turns saying the phrase, "I have the power to make wise choices."
- Repeat after me once, then let's take turns until everyone has said the phrase out loud. "I have the power to make wise choices."

Take turns until everyone is finished. As the Facilitator, it is your job to gauge the pulse of the group. If needed, add a physical affirmation like a "high five" or "fist bump" so that participants still interact with one another.

GO

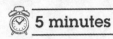 **5 minutes**

The Facilitator leads this portion of the session.

Sending participants and leaders back into their daily lives is the final step in the session. This section is meant to be simple and quick.

Say:

- Leaving this time together requires a shift. This is a safe place. This is a place where we are learning and growing together. Outside of this place are our homes, schools, families, friends, and many other social circles.
- What I want to leave you with at the end of each session is that no matter where you are in the world, no matter who you are with, God is with you on your journey.
- Let us close with prayer:

  Leader: The Lord be with you.
  Participants: And also with you.
  Leader: Let us pray.

  Holy One, God who created us to think and reason about the world around us, make us aware of your presence with us, that as we leave this place, we do so empowered to make wise choices in every aspect of our lives, through the power of the Holy Spirit. *Amen*.

AFTER·THE·SESSION
DEBRIEF

For Facilitator and Small-Group Leaders Only

Please see the full material found in Session 1, page 57.

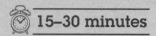 15–30 minutes

NOTES

YOU ARE THOUGHTFUL

Do not be conformed to this world, but be transformed by the renewing of your minds, so that you may discern what is the will of God—what is good and acceptable and perfect.

—Romans 12:2, *NRSV*

O heavenly Father, who hast filled the world with beauty: Open our eyes to behold thy gracious hand in all thy works; that, rejoicing in thy whole creation, we may learn to serve thee with gladness; for the sake of him through whom all things were made, thy Son Jesus Christ our Lord.[51]

....

51 Book of Common Prayer, For Joy in God's Creation, page 814

Giving young people the opportunity to explore their values in the light of the gospel of grace and love enables them to "own" those values. When they leave the protections of church or home, their values will inform their decisions and empower them to take actions that align with their values.

OBJECTIVES

- ❏ Participants will be able to explore choices for personal relationships and situations.
- ❏ Participants will consider the appropriateness of behaviors.
- ❏ Participants will consider their beliefs around and understanding of sexuality.

SUPPLIES

- ❏ pencils or pens (1 per participant)
- ❏ *These Are Our Bodies Participant Book* (1 per participant)
- ❏ *These Are Our Bodies Leader Guide* (1 for the Facilitator and 1 for each Small-Group Leader)
- ❏ HOPE[52] poster (See pp. 13–14.)
- ❏ easel paper and markers
- ❏ scrap pieces of colored paper for the Question Box (3" x 5")
- ❏ Question Box (See directions, pp. 14–17.)
- ❏ nametags
- ❏ sheets of poster board, 1 per team playing The Appropriate Game

52 The authors have done their best, without success, to track down the original source of the HOPE acronym. No copyright infringement is intended. If notified, they will gladly credit the original author in future editions of *These Are Our Bodies*.

NOTES

- ❏ blank, white index cards, 35 per team playing The Appropriate Game
- ❏ blank, colored index cards, 1 per participant, in a variety of colors
- ❏ Game Boards for The Appropriate Game (See directions, p. 192.)

PREPARATION

- ❏ Gather needed supplies. Set up the room for the session. Arrange furniture and materials so that they are readily available and designed for discussion.
- ❏ The Facilitator divides participants into groups before the session starts and assigns two Small-Group Leaders to each group. Each group should have 4–6 participants of different genders and different schools. The Facilitator will want to think about the formation of the groups to ensure that cliques are not formed. Use the nametags to delineate the groups. One group could have blue borders on the nametags and the other red. Another way is to put a different sticker on the nametags. For example you could have the star group or the happy-face group. Deciding on the groups before the session is a time saver and also makes the session go more smoothly. If you have 4–6 participants, do the following activity as one group.
- ❏ Small-Group Leaders and the Facilitator will want to read Chapters 8 and 9 in the *These Are Our Bodies Foundation Book* for additional background for today's session.

GATHER

NOTES

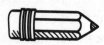

 20 minutes

As participants enter, have them put on their nametags, pick up their *Participant Books*, and select a pencil or pen.

Say:
- Welcome everyone!
- As we begin today, we must acknowledge that this is our last session together.
- I am so very proud of each one of you!
- Let us begin in the same way we did when we started back in Session 1.

HOPE Poster

Say:
- As we begin today, *(name of participant)* is going to lead us.

Participant says:
- Let's look together at our HOPE poster.
- Stand and join me as we read together:

  Honesty: We commit to sharing what we really think.
  Openness: We commit to being open to what others say, both our group members and our leaders, and most of all to God.
  Privacy: We commit to keeping what is said and done here within this space.
  Enthusiasm: We commit to laughter, fun, and a sense of wonder.

Prayer

Lead participants in this prayer:

> Holy God, one who took on flesh and lived as one of us,
> dwell with us here and give us courage to learn, grow,
>   and become more like you—
> loving, kind, and full of grace—
> through God our Creator, Christ our Redeemer,
> and the Spirit our Sustainer. *Amen*.

The Question Box

Note: Be sure you have read the full explanation of the Question Box found on pages 14–17 of the Introduction. Please see the full material found in Session 3, page 83.

Guidelines for answering questions:

> ➤ Think about the time that it will take to answer the questions. An average of 60–90 seconds per question is a reasonable guideline. Answering questions for a group of 6–8 participants will take 8–12 minutes.
> ➤ Adjust the amount of time that you allow based on your group.
> ➤ Do not over explain. Keep it moving!
> ➤ Go down the question list one by one and answer each question. The Small-Group Leaders and the Facilitator will have already decided how to answer each question and who will answer the question at the end of last session.
> ➤ Remember to answer the questions clearly and concisely. You are aiming for a 45–60 second answer.
> ➤ Don't belabor the answers. You will want to spend as much time on the session as you can.

When all the questions have been answered say:

- You all asked great questions . . . not just the ones we answered today, but those you've asked throughout the program.
- Because this is our last time to meet, we won't be writing new questions for the Question Box.
- If you do have new questions, feel free to approach any of your leaders or parents after today's session.

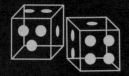

GAME

The Appropriate Game

 20 minutes

You will need one table per group for this game, preferably round. If you do not have access to this many tables, participants can sit on the floor in circles with space in the middle of each circle for the game board.

The goal of the game is for participants to decide whether a specific action or situation is appropriate for a certain age group.

Prepare the game:

Create a Game Board for each group of 4–6 people. To create a Game Board, divide a piece of poster board into six roughly equal sections. Title each section with one of these six categories: *child, tween, teen, teen sometimes, adult, never*. Create a Game Board for each team.

Create a Reference Chart for participants by copying to a sheet of easel paper (in large letters) the age range for each of the categories on the Game Board, like this:

- child (under age 10)
- tween (10–12)
- teen (13–18)
- adult (19 and above)

Create a set of Action Cards for each group. For each set of cards, write each of the following 35 actions on a separate index card:

- having a cell phone
- playing outside naked
- getting married
- going to parties
- flying on an airplane alone
- crawling on the floor
- climbing a tree

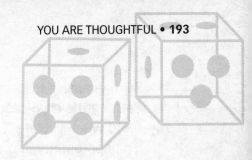

- taking a bath with a brother or sister
- having unprotected sex
- having a baby
- holding hands
- demanding your own way by crying and yelling
- watching a G-rated movie
- going to a PG-13 movie
- watching an R-rated movie without a parent
- kissing a boyfriend or girlfriend
- pressuring someone to do something they don't want to do
- going to the movies with friends
- having sexual intercourse
- petting or touching the breasts or genitals of someone else
- masturbating
- cuddling
- seeing an X-rated movie
- giving or receiving a back rub
- talking privately with someone
- texting
- spending the night alone
- spending the night with a friend of the opposite sex
- spending the night with a boyfriend or girlfriend
- talking about the intimate parts of a relationship
- gossiping about friends or acquaintances
- double dating (two couples going out together)
- going to the movies with boys and girls
- demanding that someone be your exclusive friend
- sexting (sending pictures or texts that are sexual)

Create an identical stack of these Action Cards for each group.

Play the game:

Divide participants into their small groups and assign them to their tables. Place a Game Board in the center of each table. Place a set of Action Cards—stacked and face down—on each table.

Distribute a *colored* index card to each participant. This is the participant's Decision Card. Decision Cards will be placed on the Game Board during play.

Say to participants:
- On the board in front of you are six categories. You can see on this piece of chart paper *(point to it)* how these break down. *(Review the Reference Chart.)*
- In your group, you are going to take turns drawing and reading aloud the Action Cards.
- For each action on a card, the reader must place his or her Decision Card on the Game Board, choosing at what point in someone's life that action is first appropriate to do.

- For example, if the Action Card you read says, "brush your teeth," you might put your Decision Card on the *child* section of the Game Board, because it is appropriate to start brushing your teeth when you are a child. If you put your card on *teen,* for that you would be saying that it isn't appropriate to brush your teeth until you turn 13.
- In short, pick the place on the Game Board that you think it is appropriate to do the action on the Action Card you drew.

Continue:
- Right now, we are not going to discuss the situations, just express our individual opinions. Later we will talk more about them.
- Let's begin!

Participants in each group take turns reading the Action Cards and placing their Decision Cards in response. Once all of a group's Decision Cards have been placed, they all pick them up to start a new round of the game with the next Action Cards in the stack.

Once all of the Action Cards have been read in all groups, proceed to the GRAPPLE portion of the session.

GRAPPLE

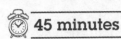
NOTES

Small-Group Leaders will want to follow along in their *Leader Guides*.

Regather the larger group, sitting together in one space, but with the small groups clustered around the room. The goal will be large-group interaction mixed with small-group interaction, whole-group questions alternating with small-group questions. Small-Group Leaders should sit with their group members.

Info for Facilitators and Small-Group Leaders:
- The sharing in today's GAME offers priceless information about participants' beliefs and understandings of life and sexuality. This is information that you could share with the parents of participants because it isn't participant-specific, but representative of the group generally.
- Parents can learn what the "pulse" is of the group and get a feel for what participants their child's age are thinking. This, in turn, can lead to expanded conversations at home about the same situations used in today's GAME.

Discuss in the *large* group:
- In The Appropriate Game we had the chance to share our opinions about when a certain action was appropriate. We did not discuss the different actions during the game because we are going to do that now.
- What situations or actions went into the *never* category? *(Share these out loud.)*
  - Why do you think some of you chose "never" for these actions?
  - Which of the actions that ended up in the category of "never" do you think should really be somewhere else? Why?
- What situations or actions went into the *adult* category. *(Share these out loud.)*

Say:

- The next few questions are for your Small-Group Leaders to ask. When you have finished discussing them, turn and look back up front so I know you are ready.

Small-Group Leaders ask these questions of their small groups:

- Some of you said *(name an action)* was for adults only. What do you think makes this appropriate only for adults?
- Think about *(name another action)*. What values in your family and in your faith helped you think about that action and when it would be appropriate?
- What situations or actions went into the *teen sometimes* category? *(Share these out loud.)*

Facilitator asks of the *large* group:

- If you feel comfortable sharing that this was your response, or if you think you know why someone else chose *teen sometimes* for this situation, why was it placed in the *teen sometimes* category?

Small-Group Leaders now ask these questions of their small groups:

- What do you think is the difference between the categories of *middle-schoolers only* and *middle-schoolers*?
- Could *(select an action from the list that participants assigned to* middle-schoolers*)* move to the *teens* category? Why or why not?
- Some of you are already 13 years old. Some of you will turn 13 very soon. Why do you think *(select any action from the list that participants assigned to* middle-schoolers*)* was mainly viewed by our group as appropriate for *middle-schoolers?*

The Facilitator now asks of the large group:

- What faith, community, or family values make *(choose an action that participants assigned to* teens*)* appropriate for middle-schoolers?
- According to what you all said, the following things were appropriate for a *tween*. *(State these aloud.)*
- This is the age group that many of you are currently in.
- How do you feel about *(select an action that participants assigned to* tweens*)* falling into the category of *tween*? *(Be sure participants express an actual feeling word, like angry, happy, upset, disappointed, etc.)*

Small-Group Leaders now ask these questions of their small groups:

- What do the actions that we think are appropriate for *tweens* have in common?
- In what ways can knowing what is appropriate for your age help prevent you from possible harm or unintended consequences?

When small groups have had a chance to discuss this last question, prepare to move on to the GUIDE portion of the session. Say:

- In just a moment we are going to transition into the GUIDE portion of our session. I want to encourage you to talk to your parents more about these situations. It is not enough to put them into an appropriate category here in our group; what you really need to know is how your parents feel about each situation. When you know how they feel, you can think it through for yourself.

GUIDE

 15 minutes

Invite all participants (Small-Group Leaders too!) to join in a large enough space where you can form a circle. After you have made the circle, invite everyone to move close enough to each other that they are touching shoulder to shoulder. Invite everyone to relax and take a deep breath. As they relax, they should naturally stop touching shoulders so closely yet maintain an appropriate level of intimacy for this portion of the session.

Invite all in the circle to close their eyes for a few seconds and slow their breathing. Maintain this for about 30 seconds.

Say:
- The title of our session today was YOU ARE THOUGHTFUL. The title was chosen because during the entire session you had to engage your brain in some serious thinking in order to make some serious choices on what was appropriate.
- Now let us shift our thoughts to why all of this matters. First, I want us to take a deep breath and relax just for a moment.

Sit in silence for about 1 minute, then continue:
- When we began our sessions together, we studied the book of Genesis and the creation story found in its pages. We learned that God declared what God had created "very good." Part of how God created human beings uniquely in God's image includes our ability to reason, or to think things through.
- For our final GUIDE time, I challenge each of you to think about why this session is so important. Consider, quietly to yourself, the answers to these questions:
  ○ Why does God care if I know what is appropriate for my life? *(Pause for silent reflection.)*
  ○ Why do my parents care if I make appropriate decisions about my life? *(Pause for silent reflection.)*
- Our God and our families care for us because they love us. God loves you unconditionally. God wants what is best in your life and what will make you most fulfilled and happy.

- To affirm each other I want us to all say the same thing, taking turns saying it to someone in the group:
  - *(Name)*, God cares for you because God loves you unconditionally and wants what is best for you.
- Repeat this sentence after me a couple of times, and then we will take turns saying it to each other.

Repeat "God cares for you because God loves you unconditionally and wants what is best for you" several times with participants. Allow time for everyone to say the phrase to the person on their right.

When all affirmations have been shared and received, continue with the GO portion of the session.

GO

 5 minutes

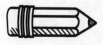

NOTES

Sending the participants and Small-Group Leaders back into their daily lives is the final step in the session. This section is meant to be simple and quick. Since this is the last session, be prepared for possible shifts in the participants. The journey to this point was long and tough. Make sure they know that though this is the end of the program, it is not the end of the opportunity to learn and grow. The adults who have walked through these sessions will remain in their lives, and their parents are a wonderful place to go when they need help.

Say:

- As I have said for nine previous sessions, leaving this time together requires a shift. This is and has been a safe place. This is a place where we are learning and growing together. Outside of this place are our homes, schools, families, friends, and many other social circles.
- What I want to leave you with at the end of each session is that no matter where you are in the world, no matter who you are with, God is with you on your journey.
- Let us close with prayer:

  Leader: The Lord be with you.
  Participants: And also with you.
  Leader: Let us pray.

Grant to us, Lord, we pray, the spirit to think and do always those things that are right, that we, who cannot exist without you, may by you be enabled to live according to your will; through Jesus Christ our Lord, who lives and reigns with you and the Holy Spirit, one God, for ever and ever.[53] *Amen*.

Leader: The Lord bless you and keep you.
Participants: Amen.
Leader: The Lord make his face to shine upon you and be gracious to you.
Participants: Amen.
Leader: The Lord lift up his countenance upon you and give you peace.
Participants: Amen.[54]

APPENDIX

SESSION 2: YOU ARE GOD'S CREATION

Puzzle Diagram

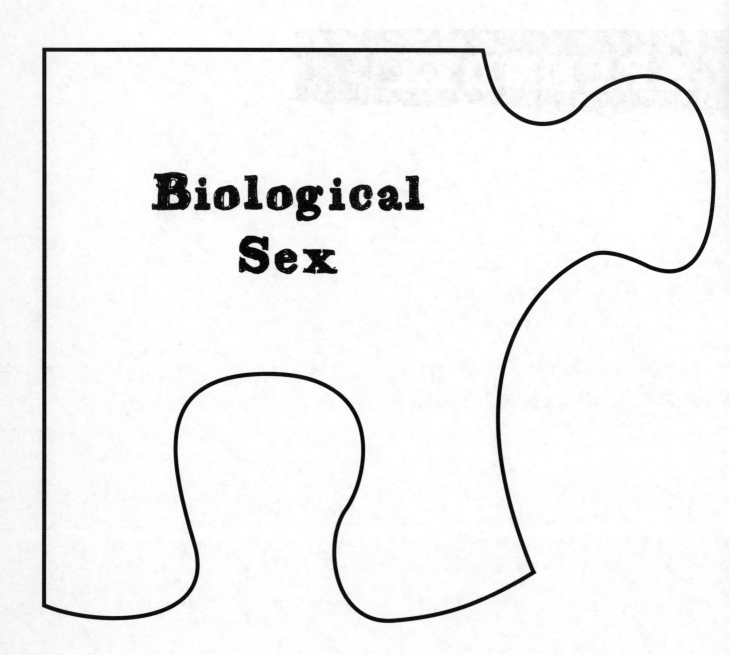

Biological Sex

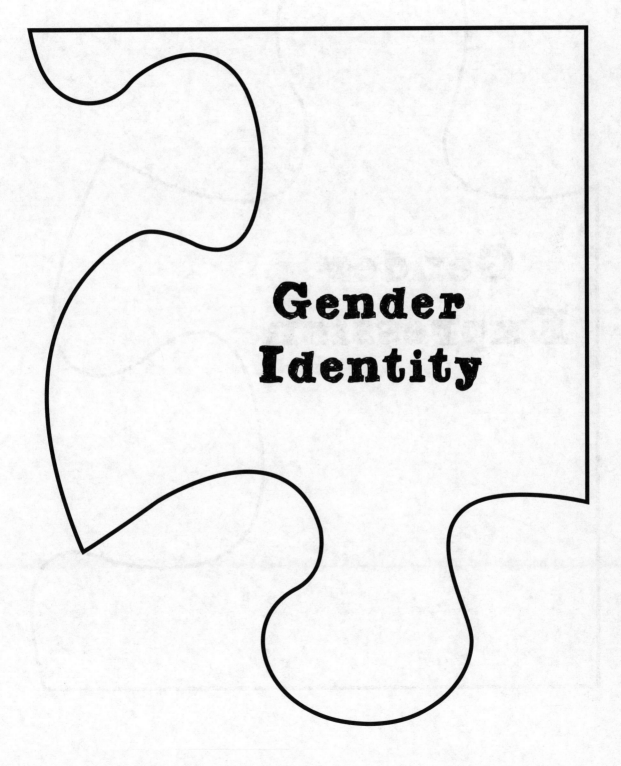

Gender
Identity

Gender Expression

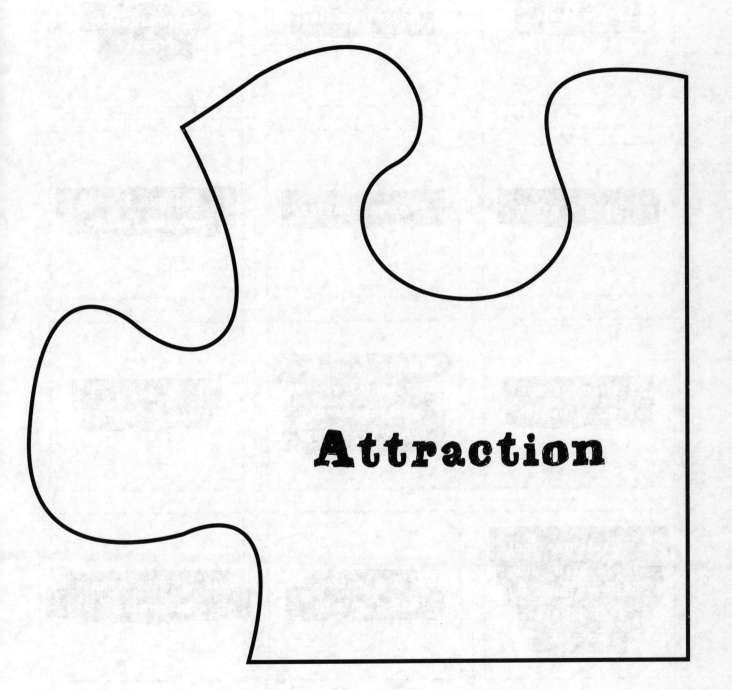

Attraction

Simple Games Cards

I am male.

I am female.

I am genetically female.

I have a penis.

I have ovaries.

I believe I am a woman inside.

I think I am a man inside.

I have thoughts about my gender apart from my body.

I do not feel like a man.

I sometimes feel like a man, but other times I feel like a woman.

I try to look feminine.

I like to dress in a masculine way.

I wear my hair like this because it makes others know I am masculine.

I don't have to dress like a boy just because I have a penis.

My wardrobe perfectly fits my self-understanding.

I like how they are polite, kind, and think of the little things.

I am interested in them.

I see their inner beauty and I am drawn to it.

I daydream about kissing them.

I get butterflies in my stomach when they are around.

Advanced Game Cards

I had a gender declared at my birth.

I produce the hormone estrogen.

I produce the hormone testosterone.

I can examine my physical anatomy to determine this.

My parents sent out birth announcements that say I am a boy because I have a penis.

I am called a girl because I have a vagina.

I have two X chromosomes.

I have an X and Y chromosome.

I claim my own gender based on how I feel.

I know I may have the body of a man, but I feel like a woman.

I struggle to fit into the gender stereotypes of my culture.

I feel like my gender is fluid.

My internal chemistry makes me feel like a man.

I may have a vagina, but I know I am a man.

When I look at myself, my body says female, but my head knows different.

I don't care what the doctors decided when I was born, I know I am a girl.

I want others to know I am feminine.

I prefer to wear masculine clothes, they are just "me."

Even if other people think I should look a certain way, I like to look like this.

I refuse to act like a boy.

I love wearing skirts.

I get called a Tomboy sometimes.

I proudly display my gender to those around me.

I am not tied down by stereotypes.

I love how they are ambitious, that is appealing to me.

I want to be with a generous person.

I am emotionally interested in them, even without the need to physically touch.

I frequently think about kissing, holding, or physically touching them.

I fantasize about them.

My body responds to their presence.

I long to experience intimacy with them.

My desires are instinctual, just part of being human.

Answer Key

Simple Game Cards

BIOLOGICAL SEX PHRASES
I am male.
I am female.
I am genetically female.
I have a penis.
I have ovaries.

GENDER IDENTITY PHRASES
I believe I am a woman inside.
I think I am a man inside.
I have thoughts about my gender apart from my body.
I do not feel like a man.
I sometimes feel like a man, but other times I feel like a woman.

GENDER EXPRESSION PHRASES
I try to look feminine.
I like to dress in a masculine way.
I wear my hair like this because it makes others know I am masculine.
I don't have to dress like a boy just because I have a penis.
My wardrobe perfectly fits my self-understanding.

ATTRACTION PHRASES
I like how they are polite, kind, and think of the little things.
I am interested in them.
I see their inner beauty and I am drawn to it.
I daydream about kissing them.
I get butterflies in my stomach when they are around.

Advanced Game Cards

BIOLOGICAL SEX PHRASES
I had a gender declared at my birth.
I produce the hormone estrogen.
I produce the hormone testosterone.
I can examine my physical anatomy to determine this.
My parents sent out birth announcements that say I am a boy because I have a penis.
I am called a girl because I have a vagina.
I have two X chromosomes.
I have an X and Y chromosome.

GENDER IDENTITY PHRASES
I claim my own gender based on how I feel.
I know I may have the body of a man, but I feel like a woman.
I struggle to fit into the gender stereotypes of my culture.
I feel like my gender is fluid.
My internal chemistry makes me feel like a man.
I may have a vagina, but I know I am a man.
When I look at myself, my body says female, but my head knows different.
I don't care what the doctors decided when I was born, I know I am a girl.

GENDER EXPRESSION PHRASES
I want others to know I am feminine.
I prefer to wear masculine clothes, they are just "me."
Even if other people think I should look a certain way, I like to look like this.
I refuse to act like a boy.
I love wearing skirts.
I get called a *Tomboy* sometimes.
I proudly display my gender to those around me.
I am not tied down by stereotypes.

ATTRACTION PHRASES
I love how they are ambitious, that is appealing to me.
I want to be with a generous person.
I am emotionally interested in them, even without the need to physically touch.
I frequently think about kissing, holding, or physically touching them.
I fantasize about them.
My body responds to their presence.
I long to experience intimacy with them.
My desires are instinctual, just part of being human.

SESSION 4: YOU ARE RELATIONAL (PART 1)

Love Strips

Love is patient.

Love is kind.

Love is not jealous.

Love does not brag.

Love is not arrogant.

Love is not rude.

Love does not seek its own advantage.

Love is not irritable.

Love does not keep a record of complaints.

Love is not happy with injustice.

Love is happy with the truth.

Love puts up with all things.

Love trusts in all things.

Love hopes for all things.

Love endures all things.

SESSION 5: YOU ARE RELATIONAL (PART 2)

Love Songs

"Best Day of My Life" by American Authors

"You Are The Best Thing" by Ray LaMontagne

"This Will Be (An Everlasting Love)" by Natalie Cole

"Sugar" by Maroon Five

"How Sweet It Is (To Be Loved By You)" by Marvin Gaye

"Happy" by Pharrell Williams

"Time of Our Lives" by Pitbull and Ne-Yo

"Feel So Close" by Calvin Harris

"I Gotta Feeling" by Black Eyed Peas

"The Way You Make Me Feel" by Michael Jackson

"Just the Way You Are" by Bruno Mars

"Can You Feel the Love Tonight" by Elton John

"In Your Eyes" by Peter Gabriel

"All I Want Is You" by U2

"I'm Yours" by Jason Mraz

"Thank You for Loving Me" by Bon Jovi

"Marry You" by Bruno Mars

"(I've Had) The Time of My Life" by Bill Medley and Jennifer Warnes

"My Best Friend" by Tim McGraw

"Make You Feel My Love" by Adele

SITUATIONS

#1 Steve and Christine have been looking into each other for several weeks now. They pretend not to notice each other. Finally, Steve called Christine and asked her to be his girlfriend. Christine said yes. After hanging up, Christine texted her friend Julie and told her she was madly in love.

#2 Antonio and Sandra have been going out together for a year. They spend time with each other's families and have even been on a few "real" dates. They like talking to each other and share many common interests. Sometimes they argue, but they keep talking until they have worked things out.

#3 Shawna met Taylor while on vacation at the beach last year. They spent lots of time together during the week at the beach and had a great time. Taylor knows that Shawna is a special person and very sweet, but after returning home from vacation their e-mails and texts became less and less frequent.

#4 Hope and Presley have been dating for 3 months. They see each other at school between classes. In the last week, Hope has felt jealous of and angry with Presley because she talks to other girls too much. Hope texts Presley several times a day to ask her what she is doing.

#5 Tim and Craig seem to always be around each other. They go to the movies together, they are on the same lacrosse team, and spend time at each other houses on the weekends. Sometimes they spend the night at each other's houses. They often study together.

#6 Susan and David enjoy all kinds of sports and have known each other for 3 years. They are also in the school band together. They are thinking about getting a part-time job at the same restaurant.

#7 Terry and Sam are neighbors and have known each other for a long time. They used to spend a lot of time together. Lately, they have hung out a couple times a month and sometimes go to the park. When they see other people on the way to the park, they stop and talk to friends and neighbors.

#8 Anna and Meg were in the same homeroom for many years. Something has changed now that they are in fewer classes together. Lately they haven't had anything to talk about.

#9 David sits in front of Amy in most of her classes. David asks Amy about homework and gets some help on group projects from Amy.

#10 Portia and Jose have dated for a while. Recently they have wanted to spend more time together. Sometimes they can't go out because of family commitments or homework. They look forward to seeing each other after school. Last week Portia and Jose had a big fight about whether one of them could go to a party without the other. Although they didn't agree, neither one is mad or angry now.

SESSION 7: YOU ARE KNOWLEDGEABLE

FACT or FICTION Answer Key

1.	Most teenagers have had sexual intercourse.	FICTION	While it is true that about ½ of all teenagers (15–19 years old) have had sexual intercourse, it is also true that about ½ have *not* had intercourse. National Survey of Family Growth (CDC) Percentage of never-married teenagers 15–19 years of age who have ever had intercourse, by age and sex: United States, 2002, 2006–2010 and 2011–2013

Female	2002	2006–2010	2011–2013
15–19 years of age	45.5%	42.6%	44.1%
15–17 years of age	30.3%	27.0%	30.2%
18–19 years of age	68.8%	62.7%	64.4%

Male	2002	2006–2010	2011–2013
15–19 years of age	45.7%	41.8%	46.8%
15–17 years of age	31.3%	28.0%	34.4%
18–19 years of age	64.3%	63.9%	64.0%

Sources:

Vital and Health Statistics, Teenagers in the United States: Sexual Activity, Contraceptive Use, and Childbearing, 2006–2010. National Survey of Family Growth, Series 23, Number 31, October 2011.

NCHS Data Brief, No. 209, July 2015 U.S. Department of Health and Human Services Centers for Disease Control and Prevention, National Center for Health Statistics. Sexual Activity, Contraceptive Use, and Childbearing of Teenagers Aged 15–19 in the United States. Gladys M. Martinez, Ph.D.; and Joyce C. Abma, Ph.D.

2.	Once a person has her first period, she can become pregnant.	FACT	When a person starts having her menstrual period, it means that her reproductive organs have begun working and that she can become pregnant. It does not mean, however, that the body is ready to have a baby. Teen mothers often deliver premature babies. To be ready to have a child involves many aspects, including readiness cognitively, psychologically, spiritually, emotionally, relationally, and economically.
3.	For a person to bathe or swim during her period is unhealthy.	FICTION	There is no reason to restrict any activity during their period.
4.	The sperm cell from the male determines the biological sex of a baby.	FACT	The sperm cell provides the genetic message that determines gender.
5.	A teenager does not need parental consent to get birth control from a clinic.	FACT & FICTION	Family planning clinics in most states don't have to tell anyone (parents included) in order to provide birth control to teenagers. However, in some states parents do have to give their consent in order for teenagers to get birth control.

6.	Sexually transmitted infections (STIs) occur without having any symptoms.	FACT	While some STIs have quite recognizable symptoms, others may not. Gonorrhea and Chlamydia, for example, display no symptoms in females and often are undetectable in males. A doctor's examination is important if a person thinks they may have an STI.
7.	If a person is not menstruating by the time she is 16, there is something wrong.	FICTION	Absolutely not. For a biologically female individual to begin having a period as early as age 8 or as late as 16 or 17 is perfectly normal. If a female is 16 and is worried because she has not yet started menstruating, she can always see a doctor to ensure everything is okay.
8.	A biologically female person can get pregnant from sex during her period.	FACT	A biologically female person can get pregnant any time during her menstrual cycle, including during her period.
9.	Birth control pills cause cancer.	FICTION	Though side effects can occur from using the pill, there is no conclusive evidence that the pill causes cancer.
10.	Only LGBTQ+ (lesbian, gay, bisexual, transgender, queer) people and drug users are at risk for HIV AIDS.	FICTION	While sex between two men and intravenous drug use remain the largest exposure categories, people infected through heterosexual contact comprise the fastest growing segment of the AIDS population.
11.	In order for sperm to be manufactured, the temperature in the testicles must be slightly cooler than normal body temperature, but not too cool.	FACT	Sperm cells can only be manufactured in the testicles when they are slightly cooler than body temperature. The scrota acts like a temperature gauge. When a biologically male body is warm the testicles are allowed to hang away from the body. When it is cold (cold air or cold water), the scrotum draws the testicles up closer to the body to keep them from being too cool.
12.	Teenagers can be treated for sexually transmitted infections without their parent's permission.	Depends	Laws vary, but most states require parental permission to provide treatment for STIs to teenagers.
13.	Alcohol and marijuana are sexual stimulants.	FICTION	There really are no sexual stimulants. Alcohol and marijuana lessen an individual's inhibitions but they do not stimulate sexual activity.
14.	There is one absolutely safe time between menstrual cycles when a biologically female individual cannot get pregnant.	FICTION	Because of the variability of the menstrual and ovulation cycle, the time when the egg is present cannot be determined exactly.
15.	Wet dreams happen to every biologically male individual.	FICTION	Some people do not have nocturnal emissions.
16.	When a rape occurs, the rapist is usually a stranger.	FICTION	The majority of rapes are perpetrated by someone known to the victim.
17.	Once an erection occurs and an individual is excited, without intercourse there can be physical harm.	FICTION	An erection is not actually painful. Erections have occurred since an individual was a fetus. An erection will go away on its own.
18.	A person can get pregnant even if their partner does not ejaculate or "come" inside of her.	FACT	A person can get pregnant even if their partner "comes" outside of her body. During foreplay, oral sex, or intercourse, semen, which contains sperm, seeps out of the penis.
19.	If a person misses her period, she is definitely pregnant.	FICTION	There are many reasons a person might miss a period. Some medications and even exercise can suppress a person's menstrual cycle.

20.	You cannot get HIV/AIDS from touching things that person with HIV/AIDS has used.	FACT	HIV/AIDS is not transmitted by casual contact like sharing drinks, or cups, hugging, kissing, or holding hands.
21.	Virginity can be proven.	FICTION	You cannot tell people's sexual histories by looking at them or by engaging in sexual activity, including sexual intercourse.
22.	People who start having sexual intercourse before the age of 16 are more likely to get pregnant than those who wait until they are over 18 to have sex.	FACT	People who have sex before they are 16 have a higher rate of pregnancy due to the lack of birth control. Many teenagers are not prepared for sexual intercourse and do not engage in "safer sex."
23.	Individuals are born with all of their eggs in their ovaries.	FACT	The eggs inside the ovaries are developed when she is a fetus inside the uterus. People do not produce more eggs over their lifetime. Although the eggs are in the ovaries as a baby and child, they are undeveloped.
24.	Oral sex is safe because you cannot get pregnant or contract STIs.	FICTION	STIs are transmitted by the touching of genital areas or mouths. Oral sex doesn't protect from STIs. An individual can get pregnant even if the partner "comes" outside of her body. During foreplay, oral sex, or intercourse, semen, which contains sperm, seeps out of the penis.
25.	There is nothing wrong with looking at pornography.	FICTION	Pornography is any sexually explicit image. Those images are a distortion of God's creation. People in pornography are seen as objects of sexual pleasure and not as children of God. We should strive to behave in such a way that shows respect for all people. Pornography is also addictive. Looking at pornography leads people to want to look at more and more sexually explicit material.
26.	Drinking alcohol leads to the same effects for adults and teenagers.	BOTH	Alcohol is a drug, a legal drug for those 21 and older. Although drinking alcohol is legal for adults and not for teenagers, there are other reasons to avoid alcohol use as a teenager. Because teens are still growing and maturing, the risks and dangers associated with alcohol use are greater for teens than for adults. Drinking alcohol negatively affects a teen's growing body and brain. Because teenagers' brains are not fully developed, their impulse control and willingness to delay gratification are not fully developed, which can lead to poor decision making. In both adults and teens, alcohol hinders decision-making skills and loosens natural inhibitions leading to risky behaviors.
27.	Consuming alcohol does not affect decision-making.	FICTION	In both adults and teens, alcohol hinders decision-making skills.
28.	Inaccurate as well as accurate information about sexuality can be found on the Internet.	FACT	The Internet can be a good resource for information and it can also provide false or incomplete information. As with any source of information, remember to "consider the source" before you believe everything that you read or hear.
29.	Masturbation is a normal part of a person's sexuality.	FACT	Although our society used to think that masturbation was "bad," we now know that masturbation is a normal part of sexuality.
30.	Drugs and alcohol do not have anything to do with sexual activity.	FICTION	The decision to engage in activity or sexual intercourse is based on judgment. Both alcohol and drugs impair judgment and loosen natural inhibitions. A person who is using alcohol or drugs may find that they do something that they normally wouldn't do, like engage in sexual activity.

SESSION 8: YOU ARE CONNECTED

GRAPPLE Interviews

For the leaders' reference while leading today's GRAPPLE, we include here the questions from the *Interview Guide* found in both the *Parent Book* and the *Participant Book*.

PARENT Interviews PARTICIPANT
Use active listening skills as you interview your child. Ask your child to describe how their faith, community, and family values influence the answers they give:
- What have you heard about dating?
- Do participants your age date?
- What do you think about that?
- What are some of the things you have seen in movies, on TV, on the Internet, or on the radio about sex?
- Do any of the things you have heard bother you?
- Do you feel like you can come to me with your questions about sexuality and sex?
- Are you comfortable with your development? Does anything worry you?
- When you think about your gender, how do you best describe yourself?
- What are three things you look for in a person to whom you are attracted?
- Is there anything you would like to share with me?

PARTICIPANT interviews PARENT
Use active listening skills as you interview your parent. Ask your parent to describe how their faith, community, and family values influence the answers they give:
- How did you learn about sex?
- Did you have sex education or family life education in school?
- Who did you talk to about sexual issues?
- Did you like the way you learned about sexuality?
- What would you have wanted to be different?
- Where do you think your values about sexuality come from? How did you learn them?
- What do you think are appropriate forms of sexual expression for someone my age who identifies as my gender?
- What do you think are appropriate forms of sexual expression for someone the same age as me but identifies as another gender than me?
- When you were my age, to whom were you attracted?
- Now that you are older, how has your attraction to others changed?

SESSION 9: YOU ARE EMPOWERED

Jeopardy Questions

REFUSAL SKILLS

100	What is one reason saying "No!" might be hard?	*You might be afraid of what they will think of you.*
200	Give two caring responses that help to say "No."	*Possibilities include:* • *That's flattering but . . .* • *It's nice of you to offer, but . . .* • *Thanks for asking, but . . .* • *I'm glad you trust me to ask, but . . .* • *I love you, but . . .* • *I like you, but . . .* • *I care about you, but . . .* • *I'm sure you have a good reason for asking, but . . .*
300	What are three ways to say "no" in this situation? A friend wants to sneak out of the house.	*Possibilities include:* • *I am uncomfortable leaving the house without telling my parents where we are going.* • *You are a great friend and I like having you over. If we sneak out, I won't be able to have you over again.*
400	Choose four good ways to say "No" from the Ways to Say . . . NO list and tell why they are helpful.	*Possibilities include:* • *I've got homework to do. (General, good excuse because there is always some homework to do.)* • *If you loved me you wouldn't keep asking. (Friends respect each other and listen when a friend says "no.")* • *It's not worth it. (Is firm and tells the other person that there is risk.)* • *I'm not comfortable. (Is honest and uses your feelings.)*
500	Describe a caring response for this situation: A friend hasn't studied for a test and asks you, "Can you let me copy off of your test?" What is your decision? What is a possible consequence? And what is an alternative that you can give your friend?	*Possibilities include:* • *I'm sure you have a good reason for asking, but no.* • *I don't let people cheat off of my tests.* • *Decision: No, the friend can't copy off the test.* • *Consequence: Both getting an "F" on the test.* • *The test is right after lunch; why don't we study during lunch and you will feel more prepared?*

SEX FOR SALE

100	What is pornography?	Any image that turns a person into a sex object, or promotes sexual relations between children and adults or links sex and violence.
200	What are some the dangers of prostitution?	Violence, poor self-esteem, physical and health problems, and legal consequences.
300	Who are prostitutes, and what are two reasons why someone might become a prostitute?	Women, men, girls, and boys can all be prostitutes. The reasons are complicated; they include needing an income, being forced into prostitution, or looking for a way out of poverty.
400	What are two main ways of making money from sex?	Prostitution and pornography.
500	What are three reasons to avoid looking at pornography?	It is addictive, it exploits people, and you can't "unsee" things.

ASSERTIVE VS. AGGRESSIVE

100	What are examples of aggressive behavior?	Gossiping (talking about other people), spreading rumors (telling stories about other people), creating or participating in groups that exclude others and influencing others to reject other people.
200	Give four results of aggressive behavior.	Aggressive behavior is damaging to relationships. Although people might get what they want in the short term, people who act aggressively damage their relationship. People who act aggressively are difficult and sometimes dangerous to be around. Often aggressive behavior can result in the arrest of the aggressor because some forms of aggressive behavior are illegal, like rape and assault. Bullying and hurting people verbally or physically is not the way that we as Christians are called to live.
300	What is assertive behavior?	Confidently strong or self-assured behavior.
400	Name some common forms of assertive behavior.	Possibilities include: • Listening to other people. • Respecting the thoughts and feeling of others. • Making "I" statements when making requests. • Using When . . ., I feel statements: When you do _____, I feel _____. • Being firm without attacking the other person.
500	What are three advantages of being assertive?	Possibilities include: • Strengthens relationships (Relationships benefit when the interests and rights of other people are respected.) • Increases interpersonal skills. • Helps one speak up when observing injustice. • Develops strong decision-making skills. • Helps one learn more about oneself. • Helps one learn to treat others with the respect that every person deserves.

STIs

100	What are STIs and two ways to get STIs?	*An STI is a Sexually Transmitted Infection.* *STIs are contracted by sexual contact and by touching survival places.*
200	What are four symptoms of STIs?	• *Unusual discharge (leaking of thick fluid) from the penis or vagina.* • *Irritation, lumps, or sores on or around the genitals.* • *Pain or tenderness in the genitals, genital area, or abdomen.* • *Painful urination or frequent need to urinate.*
300	What is the best prevention for STIs?	• *Responsible sexual behavior is the best prevention for STIs.* • *For young people, responsible sexual behavior means waiting until you are much older to become sexually active.*
400	Name four common STIs.	• *Syphilis* • *Gonorrhea* • *Chlamydia* • *Genital Herpes*
500	What do sexual contact and survival places mean in the context of STIs?	*Sexual contact: In order to pass the infection from on one body to another, there must be direct contact of STI survival places between two persons. This kind of contact generally happens during sexual activity.* *Touching of survival places: The germs that cause STIs need proper conditions to survive. Places in the body which are warm and moist, such as those found in places like the penis, vulva, rectum, or mouth provide survival places for STIs*

Tech Talk

100	What is cyber bullying?	*Bullying and aggressive behavior using technology is sometimes called cyber bullying. Cyber bullying is when people use technology like texting, e-mailing, and posting to share offensive or hurtful pictures or comments about other people.*
200	What are three ways a person can cyber bully using technology?	*Possibilities include:* • *Spreading lies and rumors about victims.* • *Sending or texting hurtful words or pictures.* • *Posting false or misleading stories to embarrass or ridicule others.* • *Forwarding or sharing personal information without permission.* • *Pretending to be other people online to trick others.* • *Spreading lies and rumors about victims.* • *Tricking people into revealing personal information.* • *Sending or forwarding mean text messages.* • *Posting pictures of victims without their consent.*
300	What should people do if they are cyber bullied?	*If you have been cyber bullied, save the messages and or pictures to show a trustworthy adult—a parent, a teacher, a counselor, or a law enforcement officer. Seek help to stop the bullying.*
400	What are three ways to stay safe online?	*Possibilities include:* • *Do not forward offensive or inappropriate messages or images.* • *Block people who share inappropriate images or words.* • *Report cyber bullying to an adult.* • *Never meet anyone in person who you only know online.* • *Don't share personal information about yourself, your friends, or your parents online.*
500	What is the grandmother test?	*If you would not want your grandmother to see what you are posting, don't post it!*

BIRTH CONTROL

100	What is abstinence and what is another name for abstinence	*Abstinence is also called* celibacy *or "saying no." It is the most effective way to not start a pregnancy. When it is used to prevent pregnancy, abstinence means not having sexual intercourse.*
200	What is birth control and is it effective?	*Birth control is any method used to prevent pregnancy. Birth control is not 100% effective, although some methods are more effective than others.*
300	What are condoms and give two facts about condoms that people should know?	*Condoms are like thick strong gloves. A condom is worn over the penis to catch the sperm so they can't enter the uterus and fallopian tubes. Condoms can be bought in a drugstore. They can only be used once then thrown away. Condoms are the only birth control that protects against contracting STIs (other than abstinence). Although condoms are effective in reducing the likelihood that an infection would be passed from one person to another, they are not 100% effective.*
400	What is "the pill"?	*Also known as "oral contraceptives," the pill is a daily medication that prevents the ovaries from releasing eggs.*
500	What is safer sex?	*Safer sex is using anything you do to prevent pregnancy and STIs. Abstinence and condom use are two ways to protect against STIs. The pill or shot are the most effective birth control methods.*

Can You Name This? Game Board for Use in the GAME

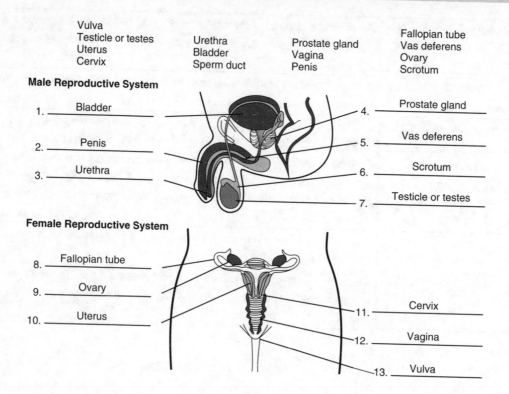

Vulva
Testicle or testes
Uterus
Cervix

Urethra
Bladder
Sperm duct

Prostate gland
Vagina
Penis

Fallopian tube
Vas deferens
Ovary
Scrotum

Male Reproductive System

1. _____ Bladder _____

2. _____ Penis _____

3. _____ Urethra _____

4. _____ Prostate gland

5. _____ Vas deferens

6. _____ Scrotum

7. _____ Testicle or testes

Female Reproductive System

8. _____ Fallopian tube _____

9. _____ Ovary _____

10. _____ Uterus _____

11. _____ Cervix

12. _____ Vagina

13. _____ Vulva

Can You Name This? Word Cards for Use in the GAME

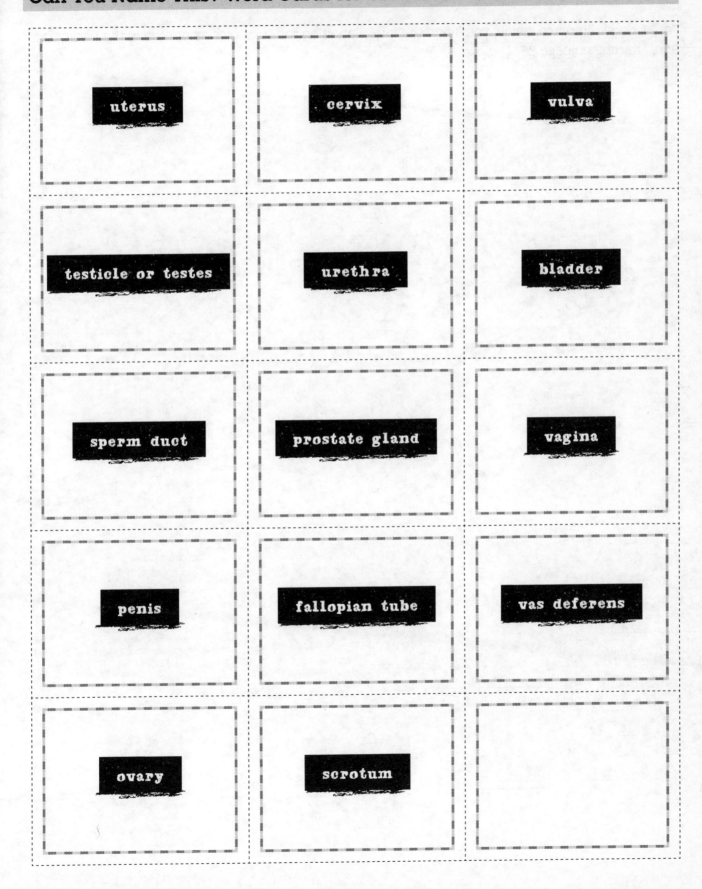

uterus

cervix

vulva

testicle or testes

urethra

bladder

sperm duct

prostate gland

vagina

penis

fallopian tube

vas deferens

ovary

scrotum

Participant Expert Info for Use in GRAPPLE

For leaders' reference, below you'll find the information on the six topics as printed in the *Participant Book* starting on page 85.

Expert Info 1: Refusal Skills

Saying "no" to your friends can be very hard sometimes. You may be afraid of what they will think of you if you don't go along with them. Here are some good ways to say "no" and still be cool.

Say something caring, for example:
- That's flattering, but . . .
- It's nice of you to offer, but . . .
- Thanks for asking, but . . .
- I'm glad you trust me to ask, but . . .
- I love you, but . . .
- I like you, but . . .
- I care about you, but . . .
- I'm sure you have a good reason for asking, but . . .

Say what the problem is, for example:
- I am not allowed to do that.
- I disagree with you.
- That is not the plan.

State your decision:
- I'd rather . . .
- I prefer . . .
- I'm going to . . .
- I'm not going to . . .
- I don't believe in . . .
- I've decided not to . . .
- I've decided to . . .

Say what the consequences are.
- I will be grounded.
- It will hurt our friendship.
- This goes against who I am.

Suggest something to do instead.
- Would you like to . . .?
- How about . . .?
- Why not . . . instead?

Options:
- If your friends insist on doing it anyway, leave.
- Try to leave the door open for them to change their minds and join you.
- You don't have to give a reason for your refusal.
- It's OK to state your reason.
- But you never have to give a reason; it only gives the person something to argue about.

Ways to say . . . NO:

- I am uncomfortable with what you are asking.
- That's my phone.
- My parents would kill me.
- It doesn't feel right.
- I don't want to.
- You're crazy.
- Let's get something to eat.
- I feel sick.
- I just want to be friends.
- I want you to leave.
- I am not ready.
- I would rather watch the game.
- Let me think about it.
- Let's go to a movie.
- I said "no" and I mean it!
- I don't know you very well.
- I have to go now.
- It is wrong.
- Don't ask me to make this choice.
- My parents are waiting up.
- Did you hear that?
- Let's stop seeing each other for a while.
- It's not worth it.
- I'm not comfortable.
- I've got homework to do.
- I have a headache.
- You're just using me.
- If you loved me you wouldn't keep asking.
- Don't make me laugh.
- If I were you, I would leave.
- You aren't listening to me.
- I can't take care of a child.
- This isn't what I had in mind.
- It is against my values.
- I'm scared.
- You are hurting my feelings.
- I think I hear my dad.
- The coach said not to.
- I don't want to mess up my hair.
- Not everyone's doing it. I'm not.
- Thanks, anyway.
- I'm too tired.
- I have a game tomorrow.
- It's past my curfew.

- I have to walk the dog.
- I thought you were different.
- Go away.
- Let's think about the consequences.
- I have to go to the bathroom.
- I have to get up early.
- My friends will be here any minute.
- Did you know that I know over 50 ways to say no?
- My stuffed animals are watching.
- Take the hint!
- Nada, never.
- I'd be sorry later.
- No!

Expert Info 2: Sex for Sale

If there is a way to make money with sex, somebody is bound to try it.

Prostitution and pornography are two examples. Prostitutes are people—women, men, girls, and boys—who are paid to perform sexual acts. Pornography is any image that exploits sexuality and misuses the gift of sex. Prostitution and pornography turn something intimate and beautiful into something that is bought and sold.

Why would someone become a prostitute?

Like so many reasons that people do things, the answer is complicated. Some prostitutes were abused as children. Some are attracted to the cash income that comes with prostitution, others see it as a way out of poverty, and some report that they would leave prostitution if they could find another job. Some people have been forced by someone more powerful to be prostitutes. We need to be careful not to stereotype people.

The lives of prostitutes are often filled with danger.

Prostitutes are frequently the victims of violence. People who pay to use a prostitute's body seldom care what happens to the prostitute. Often prostitutes are living with people who are involved with illegal drugs and can be addicted to drugs themselves.

People who pay another person for sex can experience negative consequences.

In many cities, local newspapers print the names of people who have been arrested for trying to buy the service of prostitutes. In addition to the legal consequences, people often find their lives ruined by the publicity their actions receive. Prostitution is illegal in most places. It is frequently associated with crimes of violence and drug use.

Jesus was often accused of being seen with prostitutes.

These stories are often illustrations of Jesus's compassion for all people and the difference he could make in the lives of people who had misused the gift of sexuality.

Pornography is any image that exploits human beings and misuses the gift of sexuality.

Everybody at one time or another might be curious enough to look at pictures of naked bodies. Pictures like these are widely available on the Internet or in magazines.

Pornography is any picture or image:
- that turns people into sex objects, or
- promotes sexual relations between children and adults, or
- links sex and violence.

Anytime you see people being sexuality exploited, or used as a way to make money, you are probably looking at pornography. Pornography is addictive, so it is easy to sell once a person's normal curiosity gets "hooked."

Pornography is often found on the Internet. If you see pictures or get onto a website that you know shows pornography, tell you parents immediately.

Expert Info 3: Assertive vs. Aggressive

Assertive behavior is a healthy, positive way of expressing your own needs.

Aggressive behavior is an unhealthy way of getting your way by attacking others.

Aggressive behavior is about getting the other person to do what you want them to do in a forceful or violent way. Aggressive behavior can include yelling, screaming, hitting, biting, kicking, slamming doors, and pushing. Behaviors like rape, physical attack, assault, and shooting are more serious forms of aggression that are illegal.

More common forms of aggression that you might experience include:
* yelling, threatening or frightening others
* spreading rumors
* gossiping (talking about other people), spreading rumors (telling stories about other people
* creating or participating in groups that exclude others and influencing others to reject other people

Why are some people aggressive?

People your age sometimes act aggressively because that is how they have learned to act; it can be a learned behavior. Sometimes young people have a hard time expressing their real feelings of pain, hurt, shame, or loneliness, and they use aggressive behavior to protect themselves. Some people have more complex signs of mental illness or of emotional disabilities and need the help of doctors, psychologists, and counselors.

Often aggressive behavior is called *bullying*. Bullying can describe a wide range of behavior that attacks other people. Bullying and aggressive behavior may lead to the person getting what they want in the short term, but over a longer period of time, these negative and destructive behaviors hurt their relationships.

Advantages of being assertive

Being assertive is a practice of standing up for yourself by using words and being honest about your feelings and emotions. Learning to express your own needs takes practice, but is worth the extra effort. Relationships benefit from assertive behavior that respects the interests and rights of other people. Assertive people have good interpersonal skills, they speak up when they see injustice, and they develop strong decision-making skills. Most importantly, they learn more about themselves and learn to treat others with the respect that every person deserves. In being assertive, you are demonstrating self-confidence, self-respect, and the ability to stand up for yourself effectively.

More common forms of assertive behavior that you might experience include:
- listening to other people
- respecting the thoughts and feeling of others
- making "I" statements when making requests
- using *When . . ., I feel* statements: When you do _____, I feel _____.
- being firm without attacking the other person

In our faith life, we have good examples of people who were assertive. Jesus, Martin Luther King, Jr., and Mother Teresa all stood up for what they believed and influenced others to do the same. They did not put others down or attack people to make themselves feel stronger.

Expert Info 4: STIs (Sexually Transmitted Infections)

How are STIs passed from person to person?

Sexually Transmitted Infections or STIs are passed from one person to another through sexual contact. There are more than 20 different STIs. Some of the infections that you might hear about are:

- syphilis
- gonorrhea
- chlamydia
- genital herpes

Some STIs can be treated and cured. Others are not curable, meaning that people will have the disease for life and continue to be able to pass it along to others.

What are symptoms commonly associated with STIs?

- unusual discharge (leaking of thick fluid) from the penis or vagina
- irritation, lumps, or sores on or around the genitals
- pain or tenderness in the genitals, genital area, or abdomen
- painful urination or frequent need to urinate

A person can have an STI and have no symptoms at all. Because many STIs do not have any symptoms at all, it is common for people to be infected and not be aware that they can pass on an infection. These symptoms can also indicate the presence of other diseases—diseases that are not sexually transmitted. However, people who are sexually active and have any of these symptoms are advised to see their doctor immediately.

How do you get STIs?

- You get an STI through sexual contact. In order to pass the infection from one body to another, there must be direct contact of STI survival places between two persons. This kind of contact generally happens during sexual activity.
- You can also get an STI by touching "survival places." The germs that cause STIs need proper conditions to survive. Places in the body that are warm and moist, such as those found in places like the penis, vulva, rectum, or mouth provide "survival places" for STIs.

Understand that germs live and die. Most STI germs die soon after they leave the body when they are exposed to air. It is unusual for STI to spread in ways other than human-to-human contact.

Responsible sexual behavior is the best prevention for STIs. For young people, responsible sexual behavior means waiting until you are much older to become sexually active.

Expert Info 5: Tech Talk

Bullying and aggressive behavior using technology is sometimes called *cyber bullying*. Cyber bullying is when people use technology like texting, e-mailing, and posting to share offensive or hurtful pictures or comments about other people.

Most young people will be a victim of cyber bullying. These are some of the ways that people might bully others using technology:

- send or text hurtful words or pictures
- post false or misleading stories to embarrass or ridicule others
- forward or share personal information without permission
- pretend they are other people online to trick others
- spread lies and rumors about victims
- trick people into revealing personal information
- send or forward mean text messages
- post pictures of victims without their consent

What should a person do if a victim of cyber bullying?

If you have been cyber bullied, save the messages and or pictures to show a trustworthy adult. Young people should let a trusted adult know that they are being cyber bullied—a parent, a teacher, a counselor, or law enforcement officer. Young people need help in stopping the bullying.

Stay safe online:

- Do not forward offensive or inappropriate messages or images.
- Block people who share inappropriate images or words.
- Report cyber bullying to an adult.
- Never meet anyone in person that you only know online.
- Don't share personal information about yourself, your friends, or your parents online.

Stay smart online:

- Never post or share offensive or inappropriate images or messages.
- Remember the grandmother test: If you would not want your grandmother to see what you are posting, don't post it!
- Though the Internet can feel private, it is actually very public. Never fall into the trap of believing that what you do online can only be seen by the select few friends on your list.

Expert Info 6: Birth Control

Birth Control is an easy method used to prevent pregnancy. Birth control is not 100% effective, although some methods are more effective than others.

Abstinence

Abstinence is also called *celibacy* or *"saying no."* It is the most effective way to not start a pregnancy. When it is used to prevent pregnancy, abstinence means not having sexual intercourse (not putting the penis in the vagina) and not ejaculating near the opening of the vagina. People would abstain from all sexual activity to protect against sexually transmitted infections (STIs) while using this method.

Condoms

Condoms are like thick strong gloves. A condom is worn over the penis to catch the sperm so they can't enter the uterus and fallopian tubes. Condoms can be bought in a drugstore. They can only be used once then thrown away. Condoms are the only birth control that protects against contracting STIs (other than abstinence). Although condoms are effective in reducing the likelihood that an infection would be passed from one person to another, they are not 100% effective.

The Shot

Also known as Depo-Provera or depo, the shot is made of hormones. It is given into a woman's muscle (in her arm or hip) and lasts three months. It keeps her ovaries from releasing eggs. A healthcare provider must prescribe the shot. The woman needs to get a shot every 12 weeks.

Pills

Oral contraceptives, often called "the pill," are hormones (like the ones already in her body) that keep a woman's ovaries from releasing eggs as long as she keeps taking them. A healthcare provider must prescribe them. The woman takes one pill by mouth at the same time every day (not just when she has intercourse).

IUDs

IUD stands for Intra-uterine Device. An IUD is a device that is implanted into the female's uterus in the doctor's office. This a reversible type of contraception that does not require daily medication.

The Implant

The Implant, also known as Implanon, is one small tube that is placed under the skin of a woman's upper, inner arm. It prevents pregnancy for up to 3 years by releasing a hormone that prevents her ovaries from releasing eggs. A healthcare provider must prescribe it. The woman must go to her healthcare provider's office to have it put in or removed, which only takes a few minutes.

Combining Two Methods

For extra protection, couples can combine a condom with another method of birth control (for example: birth control pills). A combination like this will help cut down the risk of pregnancy, HIV, and many other sexually transmitted infections (STIs).

Safer Sex

Many middle-schoolers have heard of safe sex, but may not know what that means. There really isn't any form of sex or sexual activity that is free from risk. The term *safer sex* is the preferred and more accurate term. Safer sex means that a couple has used protection against both pregnancy and STIs. Safer sex means using a condom to protect from STIs and an effective birth control method, like an oral contraceptive (The Pill) or The Shot. Some people think that safe sex refers to any sexual activity that cannot lead to pregnancy, like oral sex. It is not true that oral sex is safer than vaginal sex. Oral sex poses health risks as well. STIs can be spread by oral sex.